Higher
Physics
Practice Papers for SQA Exams

Paul Chambers

Mark Ramsay

Contents

The instructions and answer grid for completion of Section 1 in each practice paper can be downloaded from www.hoddereducation.co.uk/updatesandextras

HODDER GIBSON
AN HACHETTE UK COMPANY

The Publishers would like to thank the following for permission to reproduce copyright material:

Exam rubrics at the start of each practice paper; Relationships sheet and Data sheet at the start of each practice paper; CAS information in the revision grids pages v–xx reproduced by kind permission of SQA, Copyright © Scottish Qualifications Authority.

Photo credits: p. 12 © AA World Travel Library/Alamy Stock Photo

Every effort has been made to trace all copyright holders, but if any have been inadvertently overlooked the Publishers will be pleased to make the necessary arrangements at the first opportunity.

Although every effort has been made to ensure that website addresses are correct at time of going to press, Hodder Gibson cannot be held responsible for the content of any website mentioned in this book. It is sometimes possible to find a relocated web page by typing in the address of the home page for a website in the URL window of your browser.

Hachette UK's policy is to use papers that are natural, renewable and recyclable products and made from wood grown in sustainable forests. The logging and manufacturing processes are expected to conform to the environmental regulations of the country of origin.

Orders: please contact Bookpoint Ltd, 130 Park Drive, Milton Park, Abingdon, Oxon OX14 4SE. Telephone: (44) 01235 827720. Fax: (44) 01235 400454. Lines are open 9.00–5.00, Monday to Saturday, with a 24-hour message answering service. Visit our website at www.hoddereducation.co.uk. Hodder Gibson can be contacted direct on: Tel: 0141 333 4650; Fax: 0141 404 8188; email: hoddergibson@hodder.co.uk

© Paul Chambers and Mark Ramsay 2017

First published in 2017 by
Hodder Gibson, an imprint of Hodder Education,
An Hachette UK Company
211 St Vincent Street
Glasgow G2 5QY

Impression number   5 4 3 2 1
Year   2021 2020 2019 2018 2017

Cover photo © artida/123RF.com
Illustrations by Aptara, Inc.
Typeset in Din regular, 12/14.4 pts. by Aptara, Inc.
Printed in the UK

A catalogue record for this title is available from the British Library

ISBN: 978 1 5104 1506 5

Introduction

Higher Physics

The three papers included in this book provide questions and answers to support your preparation for your Higher Physics examination. They have been written to match the range and variety of questions you will face during your examination.

Design and style of the papers

The questions are of a comparable standard to those you will find on your Higher Physics paper.

Each paper is in two sections and has a total of **130** marks. In your official examination this will be scaled down to **100** marks.

Section 1: Objective test. There are **20** multiple choice items each worth 1 mark. There is only one correct answer for each question.

Section 2: This contains restricted and extended response questions totalling **110** marks. The score for this section is then scaled down to **80** marks and this is combined with your score for the multiple choice section to give a total out of **100**.

For example, if you scored 14 for your multiple choice and 75 for section 2, this would be scaled down as follows:

$$14 + (75 \times 80/110); 14 + 55 = 69$$

This score would then be added to your assignment to give a score out of 120. It is this mark which will determine the grade you receive. You can see from this that 1 mark from section 1 is worth more than 1 mark from section 2.

Each paper has been written to reflect the balance of the topics as they are described in the guidance documentation for teachers.

The three topics are:

- Our Dynamic Universe (ODU)
- Particles and Waves (P&W)
- Electricity and Energy (E&E).

In the Higher Physics exam, students will be expected to demonstrate their skills, knowledge and understanding of physics by

- making statements, describing information, providing explanations and integrating knowledge
- applying knowledge of physics to new situations, interpreting information and solving problems
- planning and designing experiments/practical investigations to test given hypotheses or to illustrate particular effects, including safety measures

- selecting information and presenting information appropriately in a variety of forms
- processing information (using calculations, significant figures and units, where appropriate)
- making predictions from evidence/information
- drawing valid conclusions and giving explanations supported by evidence/justification
- evaluating experimental procedures, identifying sources of uncertainty and suggesting improvements.

The papers attempt to match the range and challenge across the grades that you will experience in your examination.

Revision grids

The revision grids on pages v–xx match each question to the coursework being assessed. The Course Assessment Specification (CAS) identifies the mandatory knowledge and key areas within the course. Each question is linked to the relevant part in a key area which is being assessed. Each part has been numbered to allow the exact section of a key area to be identified. You can use this to determine your confidence across all the areas of the course.

The question pages have student margins and these indicate where the topic covered in the question can be found in the accompanying Hodder Gibson book *How to Pass Higher Physics* (HTP). They also indicate the relevant area of the Course Assessment Specification (CAS) as shown in the revision grids.

Answers

The answers give a 'standard' response or expected answer to the question. There are, however, questions which have more than one response or acceptable way of being answered. Open-ended questions in particular are clear examples of these.

Where appropriate there are small explanations of why this value was chosen. For example, at the top of a projectile's flight it may be highlighted that at this point the vertical velocity is briefly zero. Some questions do not lend themselves to added explanations of this type.

Examination practice

The Higher Physics examination is 2 hours 30 minutes in duration. You have to attempt **130** marks in **150** minutes. As you can see, this equates to approximately one minute per mark. It is, however, difficult to adhere to this in an exam situation. A multiple choice question involving recall or a simple calculation may take only seconds. A question that requires you to explain complex phenomena but is allocated 2 marks will take much longer. As a guide, try to allocate your time to groups of total marks of around 10 or so. In other words, you should be near the end of a 10 mark question in about 10 minutes. Use these papers to help you get to the appropriate pace.

Where possible, show your working to increase your opportunity of being awarded marks. Marks are given for correct physics, the selection of the correct relationship, correct substitution of values into formulae, correct calculations and a statement of the correct answer with the correct unit.

Include units in your final answers, ensure answers are to an appropriate number of significant figures and then move on to the next section.

Revision grids

Unit 1: Our Dynamic Universe

Key area	Paper A		Paper B		Paper C		Date completed
	Section 1	Section 2	Section 1	Section 2	Section 1	Section 2	
ODU 1.1 Equations of motion for objects moving with constant acceleration in a straight line	2	2 a)				1	
ODU 1.2 Motion–time graphs for motion with constant acceleration in a straight line	1 3	1 a)	3	1 b) iv)		2 c)	
ODU 1.3 Displacement–, velocity– and acceleration–time graphs and their interrelationships	1 3	1 a)				2 c)	
ODU 1.4 Graphs for bouncing objects and objects thrown vertically upwards					1	2 a), 2 b)	
ODU 1.5 All graphs restricted to constant acceleration in one dimension, inclusive of change of direction			3	2			
ODU 2.1 Balanced and unbalanced forces; the effects of friction; terminal velocity	4	1 a)		1 2 b)			
ODU 2.2 Forces acting in one plane only			7	5 2 a)			

Key area	Paper A		Paper B		Paper C		Date completed
	Section 1	Section 2	Section 1	Section 2	Section 1	Section 2	
ODU 2.3 Analysis of motion using Newton's first and second laws; frictional force as a negative vector quantity; no reference to static and dynamic friction		2 b)		1 5 c)			
ODU 2.4 Tension as a pulling force exerted by a string or cable on another object		2 c)	7	5 a), 5 b)			
ODU 2.5 Velocity–time graph of a falling object when air resistance is taken into account, including the effect of changing the surface area of the falling object					2		
ODU 2.6 Resolving a force into two perpendicular components	5					3 a)	
ODU 2.7 Forces acting at an angle to the direction of movement					3	3 b)	
ODU 2.8 Resolving the weight of an object on a slope into a component acting down the slope and a component acting normal to the slope	5		2 8				
ODU 2.9 Systems of balanced forces with forces acting in two dimensions						3 c), 3 d)	
ODU 2.10 Work done, potential energy, kinetic energy and power in familiar and unfamiliar situations		1 b), 1 c)	4	1 a) ii)	4		

Key area	Paper A		Paper B		Paper C		Date completed
	Section 1	Section 2	Section 1	Section 2	Section 1	Section 2	
ODU 2.11 Conservation of energy		1 b), 1 c)	1	1	4		
ODU 3.1 Conservation of momentum in one dimension and in cases where the objects may move in opposite directions	6	3 a)		1 a) i)			
ODU 3.2 Kinetic energy in elastic and inelastic collisions		3 b)		4			
ODU 3.3 Explosions and Newton's third law					5		
ODU 3.4 Conservation of momentum in explosions in one dimension only							
ODU 3.5 Force–time graphs during contact of colliding objects			5				
ODU 3.6 Impulse found from the area under a force–time graph			5				
ODU 3.7 Equivalence of change in momentum and impulse		3 c)		1 2 c), 2 d), 2 e)			
ODU 3.8 Newton's third law of motion							
ODU 4.1 Projectiles and satellites		4 a)		1 b) iii) 2 3 b)			
ODU 4.2 Resolving the motion of a projectile with an initial velocity into horizontal and vertical components and their use in calculations		4 a)		1 b) i), ii)	6		

Key area	Paper A		Paper B		Paper C		Date completed
	Section 1	Section 2	Section 1	Section 2	Section 1	Section 2	
ODU 4.3 Comparison of projectiles with objects in free fall		4 c)					
ODU 4.4 Gravitational field strength of planets, natural satellites and stars; calculating the force exerted on objects placed in a gravitational field	7	4 b)		3 a)		4	
ODU 4.5 Newton's Universal Law of Gravitation						4	
ODU 5.1 The speed of light in a vacuum is the same for all observers					7		
ODU 5.2 The constancy of the speed of light led Einstein to postulate that measurements of space and time for a moving observer are changed relative to those for a stationary observer							
ODU 5.3 Length contraction and time dilation		5					
ODU 6.1 The Doppler effect is observed in sound and light		6	6				
ODU 6.2 The Doppler effect causes shifts in wavelengths of sound and light. The light from objects moving away from us is shifted to longer (more red) wavelengths		6					

Key area	Paper A		Paper B		Paper C		Date completed
	Section 1	Section 2	Section 1	Section 2	Section 1	Section 2	
ODU 6.3 The red-shift of a galaxy is the change in wavelength divided by the emitted wavelength. For slowly moving galaxies, red-shift is the ratio of the velocity of the galaxy to the velocity of light					8		
ODU 6.4 Hubble's law shows the relationship between the recession velocity of a galaxy and its distance from us				12 a), 12 b)		5	
ODU 6.5 Hubble's law allows us to estimate of the age of the Universe				12 c), 12 d)		5	
ODU 6.6 Evidence for the expanding Universe							
ODU 6.7 We can estimate the mass of a galaxy by the orbital speed of stars within it					9		
ODU 6.8 Evidence for dark matter from observations of the mass of galaxies					15		
ODU 6.9 Evidence for dark energy from the accelerating rate of expansion of the Universe							

Key area	Paper A		Paper B		Paper C		Date completed
	Section 1	Section 2	Section 1	Section 2	Section 1	Section 2	
ODU 6.10 The temperature of stellar objects is related to the distribution of emitted radiation over a wide range of wavelengths. The wavelength of the peak of this distribution is shorter for hotter objects than for cooler objects	8					6 a), 6 b) i)	
ODU 6.11 Qualitative relationship between radiation per unit surface area and temperature of a star							
ODU 6.12 Cosmic microwave background radiation as evidence for the Big Bang and subsequent expansion of the Universe						6 b) ii)	

Unit 2: Particles & Waves

Key area	Paper A		Paper B		Paper C		Date completed
	Section 1	Section 2	Section 1	Section 2	Section 1	Section 2	
P&W 1.1 Orders of magnitude: the range of orders of magnitude of length from the very small (sub-nuclear) to the very large (distance to furthest known celestial objects)	9						
P&W 1.2 The standard model of fundamental particles and interactions							

Key area	Paper A		Paper B		Paper C		Date completed
	Section 1	Section 2	Section 1	Section 2	Section 1	Section 2	
P&W 1.3 Evidence for the sub-nuclear particles and the existence of antimatter							
P&W 1.4 Fermions, the matter particles, consist of quarks (six types) and leptons (electron, muon and tau, together with their neutrinos)					10		
P&W 1.5 Hadrons are composite particles made of quarks. Baryons are made of three quarks and mesons are made of two quarks		7	12		10		
P&W 1.6 The force-mediating particles are bosons (photons, W and Z bosons, and gluons)					10		
P&W 1.7 Description of beta decay as the first evidence for the neutrino	10					7	
P&W 2.1 Fields exist around charged particles and between charged parallel plates							
P&W 2.2 Examples of electric field patterns for single point charges, systems of two point charges and between parallel plates	11						
P&W 2.3 Movement of charged particles in an electric field				7 b)	12		

Key area	Paper A		Paper B		Paper C		Date completed
	Section 1	Section 2	Section 1	Section 2	Section 1	Section 2	
P&W 2.4 The relationship between potential difference, work and charge gives the definition of the volt	12						
P&W 2.5 Calculation of the speed of a charged particle accelerated by an electric field			11	6 c), 6 d) 7 a)	10		
P&W 2.6 A moving charge produces a magnetic field			14				
P&W 2.7 The determination of the direction of the force on a charged particle moving in a magnetic field for negative and positive charges (right-hand rule for negative charges)	13						
P&W 2.8 Basic operation of particle accelerators in terms of acceleration, deflection and collision of charged particles				6 a), 6 b)			
P&W 3.1 Nuclear equations to describe radioactive decay, fission and fusion reactions with reference to mass and energy equivalence, including calculations		8		8			
P&W 3.2 Coolant and containment issues in nuclear fission and fusion reactors							

Key area	Paper A		Paper B		Paper C		Date completed
	Section 1	Section 2	Section 1	Section 2	Section 1	Section 2	
P&W 4.1 Photoelectric effect as evidence for the particulate nature of light					11	8	
P&W 4.2 Photons of sufficient energy can eject electrons from the surface of materials						8	
P&W 4.3 The threshold frequency is the minimum frequency of a photon required for photoemission		9	13			8	
P&W 4.4 The work function of the material is the minimum energy required to cause photoemission		9	13			8	
P&W 4.5 Determination of the maximum kinetic energy of photoelectrons							
P&W 5.1 Conditions for constructive and destructive interference			9				
P&W 5.2 Coherent waves have a constant phase relationship and have the same frequency, wavelength and velocity. Constructive and destructive interference in terms of phase between two waves	14						
P&W 5.3 Interference of waves using two coherent sources						9	

Key area	Paper A		Paper B		Paper C		Date completed
	Section 1	Section 2	Section 1	Section 2	Section 1	Section 2	
P&W 5.4 Maxima and minima are produced when the path difference between waves is a whole number of wavelengths or an odd number of half wavelengths, respectively		10	9				
P&W 5.5 The relationship between the wavelength, distance between the sources, distance from the sources and the spacing between maxima or minima		10		11			
P&W 5.6 The relationship between the grating spacing, wavelength and angle to the maxima		10		11	18		
P&W 6.1 Absolute refractive index of a material is the ratio of the sine of the angle of incidence in vacuum (air) to the sine of the angle of refraction in the material. Refractive index of air treated as the same as that of a vacuum	15		15	10			
P&W 6.2 Situations where light travels from a more dense to a less dense medium/material				10			

Key area	Paper A		Paper B		Paper C		Date completed
	Section 1	Section 2	Section 1	Section 2	Section 1	Section 2	
P&W 6.3 Refractive index can also be found from the ratio of speed of light in vacuum (air) to the speed in the material and the ratio of the wavelengths					16		
P&W 6.4 Variation of refractive index with frequency			16				
P&W 6.5 Critical angle and total internal reflection		11					
P&W 7.1 Irradiance and the inverse square law	16				14	11	
P&W 7.2 Irradiance is power per unit area					14	11	
P&W 7.3 The relationship between irradiance and distance from a point light source					14	11	
P&W 7.4 Line and continuous emission spectra, absorption spectra and energy level transitions						12	
P&W 7.5 The Bohr model of the atom		12					
P&W 7.6 Movement of electrons between energy levels		12					
P&W 7.7 The terms ground state, energy levels, ionisation and zero potential energy for the Bohr model of the atom		12					

Key area	Paper A		Paper B		Paper C		Date completed
	Section 1	Section 2	Section 1	Section 2	Section 1	Section 2	
P&W 8.1 Emission of photons due to movement of electrons between energy levels and dependence of photon frequency on energy difference between levels		12			17		
P&W 8.2 The relationship between photon energy, Planck's constant and photon frequency		12			17		
P&W 8.3 Absorption lines in the spectrum of sunlight provide evidence for the composition of the Sun's upper atmosphere			20				

Unit 3: Electricity & Energy

Key area	Paper A		Paper B		Paper C		Date completed
	Section 1	Section 2	Section 1	Section 2	Section 1	Section 2	
E&E 1.1 a.c. as a current which changes direction and instantaneous value with time							
E&E 1.2 Calculations involving peak and r.m.s. values	17	13	19				
E&E 1.3 Determination of frequency from graphical data		13	17				

Key area	Paper A		Paper B		Paper C		Date completed
	Section 1	Section 2	Section 1	Section 2	Section 1	Section 2	
E&E 2.1 Use relationships involving potential difference, current, resistance and power to analyse circuits; calculations may involve several steps						14	
E&E 2.2 Calculations involving potential divider circuits			10				
E&E 3.1 Electromotive force, internal resistance and terminal potential difference; ideal supplies, short circuits and open circuits		14		9 a), 9 b), 9 c)			
E&E 3.2 Determining internal resistance and electromotive force using graphical analysis		14				13	
E&E 4.1 Capacitors and the relationship between capacitance, charge and potential difference							
E&E 4.2 The total energy stored in a charged capacitor is the area under the charge against potential difference graph. Use the relationships between energy, charge, capacitance and potential difference	18		18	9 d), 9 e)	19		

Key area	Paper A		Paper B		Paper C		Date completed
	Section 1	Section 2	Section 1	Section 2	Section 1	Section 2	
E&E 4.3 Variation of current and potential difference against time for both charging and discharging				9 f), 9 g)			
E&E 4.4 The effect of resistance and capacitance on charging and discharging curves				9			
E&E 5.1 Solids can be categorised into conductors, semiconductors or insulators by their ability to conduct electricity							
E&E 5.2 The electrons in atoms are contained in energy levels. When the atoms come together to form solids, the electrons then become contained in energy bands separated by gaps	19						
E&E 5.3 In metals the highest occupied band is not completely full and this allows the electrons to move and therefore conduct. This band is known as the conduction band							

Key area	Paper A		Paper B		Paper C		Date completed
	Section 1	Section 2	Section 1	Section 2	Section 1	Section 2	
E&E 5.4 In an insulator the highest occupied band (called the valence band) is full. The first unfilled band above the valence band is the conduction band. For an insulator the gap between the valence band and the conduction band is large and at room temperature there is not enough energy available to move electrons from the valence band into the conduction band where they would be able to contribute to conduction. There is no electrical conduction in an insulator	19						
E&E 5.5 In a semiconductor the gap between the valence band and conduction band is smaller and at room temperature there is sufficient energy available to move some electrons from the valence band into the conduction band allowing some conduction to take place. An increase in temperature increases the conductivity of a semiconductor					13		

Key area	Paper A		Paper B		Paper C		Date completed
	Section 1	Section 2	Section 1	Section 2	Section 1	Section 2	
E&E 5.6 During manufacture, the conductivity of semiconductors can be controlled, resulting in two types: p-type and n-type							
E&E 5.7 When p-type and n-type materials are joined, a layer is formed at the junction. The electrical properties of this layer are used in a number of devices	20						
E&E 5.8 Solar cells are p-n junctions designed so that a potential difference is produced when photons enter the layer. This is the photovoltaic effect							
E&E 5.9 LEDs are p-n junctions which emit photons when a current is passed through the junction							

Relationships sheet

You will be provided with a Relationships sheet in your final exam. Please refer to it as required for each practice paper.

$$d = \bar{v}t$$

$$s = \bar{v}t$$

$$v = u + at$$

$$s = ut + \frac{1}{2}at^2$$

$$v^2 = u^2 + 2as$$

$$s = \frac{1}{2}(u + v)t$$

$$W = mg$$

$$F = ma$$

$$E_W = Fd$$

$$E_p = mgh$$

$$E_k = \frac{1}{2}mv^2$$

$$P = \frac{E}{t}$$

$$p = mv$$

$$Ft = mv - mu$$

$$F = G\frac{m_1 m_2}{r^2}$$

$$t' = \frac{t}{\sqrt{1 - \left(\frac{v}{c}\right)^2}}$$

$$l' = l\sqrt{1 - \left(\frac{v}{c}\right)^2}$$

$$f_o = f_s\left(\frac{v}{v \pm v_s}\right)$$

$$z = \frac{\lambda_{observed} - \lambda_{rest}}{\lambda_{rest}}$$

$$z = \frac{v}{c}$$

$$v = H_0 d$$

$$W = QV$$

$$E = mc^2$$

$$E = hf$$

$$E_k = hf - hf_0$$

$$E_2 - E_1 = hf$$

$$T = \frac{1}{f}$$

$$v = f\lambda$$

$$d \sin \theta = m\lambda$$

$$n = \frac{\sin \theta_1}{\sin \theta_2}$$

$$\frac{\sin \theta_1}{\sin \theta_2} = \frac{\lambda_1}{\lambda_2} = \frac{v_1}{v_2}$$

$$\sin \theta_c = \frac{1}{n}$$

$$I = \frac{k}{d^2}$$

$$I = \frac{P}{A}$$

path difference $= m\lambda$ or $\left(m + \frac{1}{2}\right)\lambda$ where $m = 0, 1, 2 \ldots$

$$\text{random uncertainty} = \frac{\text{max. value} - \text{min. value}}{\text{number of values}}$$

$$V_{peak} = \sqrt{2}V_{rms}$$

$$I_{peak} = \sqrt{2}I_{rms}$$

$$Q = It$$

$$V = IR$$

$$P = IV = I^2 R = \frac{V^2}{R}$$

$$R_T = R_1 + R_2 + \ldots$$

$$\frac{1}{R_T} = \frac{1}{R_1} + \frac{1}{R_2} + \ldots$$

$$E = V + Ir$$

$$V_1 = \left(\frac{R_1}{R_1 + R_2}\right)V_s$$

$$\frac{V_1}{V_2} = \frac{R_1}{R_2}$$

$$C = \frac{Q}{V}$$

$$E = \frac{1}{2}QV = \frac{1}{2}CV^2 = \frac{1}{2}\frac{Q^2}{C}$$

Additional relationships

Circle

circumference = $2\pi r$

area = πr^2

Sphere

area = $4\pi r^2$

volume = $\dfrac{4}{3}\pi r^3$

Trigonometry

$\sin \theta = \dfrac{\text{opposite}}{\text{hypotenuse}}$

$\cos \theta = \dfrac{\text{adjacent}}{\text{hypotenuse}}$

$\tan \theta = \dfrac{\text{opposite}}{\text{adjacent}}$

$\sin^2 \theta + \cos^2 \theta = 1$

Electron Arrangements of Elements

Key

Atomic number
Symbol
Electron arrangement
Name

Transition Elements

Group 1

Atomic number	Symbol	Electron arrangement	Name
1	H	1	Hydrogen
3	Li	2,1	Lithium
11	Na	2,8,1	Sodium
19	K	2,8,8,1	Potassium
37	Rb	2,8,18,8,1	Rubidium
55	Cs	2,8,18,18,8,1	Caesium
87	Fr	2,8,18,32,18,8,1	Francium

Group 2

Atomic number	Symbol	Electron arrangement	Name
4	Be	2,2	Beryllium
12	Mg	2,8,2	Magnesium
20	Ca	2,8,8,2	Calcium
38	Sr	2,8,18,8,2	Strontium
56	Ba	2,8,18,18,8,2	Barium
88	Ra	2,8,18,32,18,8,2	Radium

Transition Elements (Groups 3–12)

Group	Period 4	Period 5	Period 6	Period 7
(3)	21 **Sc** 2,8,9,2 Scandium	39 **Y** 2,8,18,9,2 Yttrium	57 **La** 2,8,18,18,9,2 Lanthanum	89 **Ac** 2,8,18,32,18,9,2 Actinium
(4)	22 **Ti** 2,8,10,2 Titanium	40 **Zr** 2,8,18,10,2 Zirconium	72 **Hf** 2,8,18,32,10,2 Hafnium	104 **Rf** 2,8,18,32,32,10,2 Rutherfordium
(5)	23 **V** 2,8,11,2 Vanadium	41 **Nb** 2,8,18,12,1 Niobium	73 **Ta** 2,8,18,32,11,2 Tantalum	105 **Db** 2,8,18,32,32,11,2 Dubnium
(6)	24 **Cr** 2,8,13,1 Chromium	42 **Mo** 2,8,18,13,1 Molybdenum	74 **W** 2,8,18,32,12,2 Tungsten	106 **Sg** 2,8,18,32,32,12,2 Seaborgium
(7)	25 **Mn** 2,8,13,2 Manganese	43 **Tc** 2,8,18,13,2 Technetium	75 **Re** 2,8,18,32,13,2 Rhenium	107 **Bh** 2,8,18,32,32,13,2 Bohrium
(8)	26 **Fe** 2,8,14,2 Iron	44 **Ru** 2,8,18,15,1 Ruthenium	76 **Os** 2,8,18,32,14,2 Osmium	108 **Hs** 2,8,18,32,32,14,2 Hassium
(9)	27 **Co** 2,8,15,2 Cobalt	45 **Rh** 2,8,18,16,1 Rhodium	77 **Ir** 2,8,18,32,15,2 Iridium	109 **Mt** 2,8,18,32,32,15,2 Meitnerium
(10)	28 **Ni** 2,8,16,2 Nickel	46 **Pd** 2,8,18,18,0 Palladium	78 **Pt** 2,8,18,32,17,1 Platinum	110 **Ds** 2,8,18,32,32,17,1 Darmstadtium
(11)	29 **Cu** 2,8,18,1 Copper	47 **Ag** 2,8,18,18,1 Silver	79 **Au** 2,8,18,32,18,1 Gold	111 **Rg** 2,8,18,32,32,18,1 Roentgenium
(12)	30 **Zn** 2,8,18,2 Zinc	48 **Cd** 2,8,18,18,2 Cadmium	80 **Hg** 2,8,18,32,18,2 Mercury	112 **Cn** 2,8,18,32,32,18,2 Copernicium

Groups 3–7 and Group 0

Group 3 (13)	Group 4 (14)	Group 5 (15)	Group 6 (16)	Group 7 (17)	Group 0 (18)
					2 **He** 2 Helium
5 **B** 2,3 Boron	6 **C** 2,4 Carbon	7 **N** 2,5 Nitrogen	8 **O** 2,6 Oxygen	9 **F** 2,7 Fluorine	10 **Ne** 2,8 Neon
13 **Al** 2,8,3 Aluminium	14 **Si** 2,8,4 Silicon	15 **P** 2,8,5 Phosphorus	16 **S** 2,8,6 Sulfur	17 **Cl** 2,8,7 Chlorine	18 **Ar** 2,8,8 Argon
31 **Ga** 2,8,18,3 Gallium	32 **Ge** 2,8,18,4 Germanium	33 **As** 2,8,18,5 Arsenic	34 **Se** 2,8,18,6 Selenium	35 **Br** 2,8,18,7 Bromine	36 **Kr** 2,8,18,8 Krypton
49 **In** 2,8,18,18,3 Indium	50 **Sn** 2,8,18,18,4 Tin	51 **Sb** 2,8,18,18,5 Antimony	52 **Te** 2,8,18,18,6 Tellurium	53 **I** 2,8,18,18,7 Iodine	54 **Xe** 2,8,18,18,8 Xenon
81 **Tl** 2,8,18,32,18,3 Thallium	82 **Pb** 2,8,18,32,18,4 Lead	83 **Bi** 2,8,18,32,18,5 Bismuth	84 **Po** 2,8,18,32,18,6 Polonium	85 **At** 2,8,18,32,18,7 Astatine	86 **Rn** 2,8,18,32,18,8 Radon

Lanthanides

Atomic number	Symbol	Electron arrangement	Name
57	La	2,8,18,18,9,2	Lanthanum
58	Ce	2,8,18,20,8,2	Cerium
59	Pr	2,8,18,21,8,2	Praseodymium
60	Nd	2,8,18,22,8,2	Neodymium
61	Pm	2,8,18,23,8,2	Promethium
62	Sm	2,8,18,24,8,2	Samarium
63	Eu	2,8,18,25,8,2	Europium
64	Gd	2,8,18,25,9,2	Gadolinium
65	Tb	2,8,18,27,8,2	Terbium
66	Dy	2,8,18,28,8,2	Dysprosium
67	Ho	2,8,18,29,8,2	Holmium
68	Er	2,8,18,30,8,2	Erbium
69	Tm	2,8,18,31,8,2	Thulium
70	Yb	2,8,18,32,8,2	Ytterbium
71	Lu	2,8,18,32,9,2	Lutetium

Actinides

Atomic number	Symbol	Electron arrangement	Name
89	Ac	2,8,18,32,18,9,2	Actinium
90	Th	2,8,18,32,18,10,2	Thorium
91	Pa	2,8,18,32,20,9,2	Protactinium
92	U	2,8,18,32,21,9,2	Uranium
93	Np	2,8,18,32,22,9,2	Neptunium
94	Pu	2,8,18,32,24,8,2	Plutonium
95	Am	2,8,18,32,25,8,2	Americium
96	Cm	2,8,18,32,25,9,2	Curium
97	Bk	2,8,18,32,27,8,2	Berkelium
98	Cf	2,8,18,32,28,8,2	Californium
99	Es	2,8,18,32,29,8,2	Einsteinium
100	Fm	2,8,18,32,30,8,2	Fermium
101	Md	2,8,18,32,31,8,2	Mendelevium
102	No	2,8,18,32,32,8,2	Nobelium
103	Lr	2,8,18,32,32,9,2	Lawrencium

Higher
Physics

Data sheet

Common physical quantities

Quantity	Symbol	Value	Quantity	Symbol	Value
Speed of light in vacuum	c	$3.00 \times 10^8 \, \text{m s}^{-1}$	Planck's constant	h	$6.63 \times 10^{-34} \, \text{J s}$
Magnitude of the charge on an electron	e	$1.60 \times 10^{-19} \, \text{C}$	Mass of electron	m_e	$9.11 \times 10^{-31} \, \text{kg}$
Universal Constant of Gravitation	G	$6.67 \times 10^{-11} \, \text{m}^3 \, \text{kg}^{-1} \, \text{s}^{-2}$	Mass of neutron	m_n	$1.675 \times 10^{-27} \, \text{kg}$
Gravitational acceleration on Earth	g	$9.8 \, \text{m s}^{-2}$	Mass of proton	m_p	$1.673 \times 10^{-27} \, \text{kg}$
Hubble's constant	H_0	$2.3 \times 10^{-18} \, \text{s}^{-1}$			

Refractive indices

The refractive indices refer to sodium light of wavelength 589 nm and to substances at a temperature of 273 K.

Substance	Refractive index	Substance	Refractive index
Diamond	2·42	Water	1·33
Crown glass	1·50	Air	1·00

Spectral lines

Element	Wavelength/nm	Colour	Element	Wavelength/nm	Colour
Hydrogen	656	Red	Cadmium	644	Red
	486	Blue-green		509	Green
	434	Blue-violet		480	Blue
	410	Violet			
	397	Ultraviolet	Lasers		
	389	Ultraviolet	Element	Wavelength/nm	Colour
			Carbon dioxide	9550 } 10590 }	Infrared
Sodium	589	Yellow	Helium-neon	633	Red

Properties of selected materials

Substance	Density/kg m^{-3}	Melting Point/K	Boiling Point/K
Aluminium	2.70×10^3	933	2623
Copper	8.96×10^3	1357	2853
Ice	9.20×10^2	273	. . . .
Sea Water	1.02×10^3	264	377
Water	1.00×10^3	273	373
Air	1·29	. . . .	. . . .
Hydrogen	9.0×10^{-2}	14	20

The gas densities refer to a temperature of 273 K and a pressure of $1.01 \times 10^5 \, \text{Pa}$.

Duration – 2 hours and 30 minutes

Total marks – 130

SECTION 1 – 20 marks

Attempt ALL questions.

SECTION 2 – 110 marks

Attempt ALL questions.

Reference may be made to the Data sheet on page 2 and to the Relationships sheet.

Care should be taken to give an appropriate number of significant figures in the final answers to calculations.

Write your answers clearly in the spaces provided in this paper. Any rough work must be written in this paper. You should score through your rough work when you have written your final copy.

Use **blue** or **black** ink.

A

Section 1

SECTION 1 – 20 MARKS

Attempt ALL questions – instructions/answer grid available at www.hoddereducation.co.uk/updatesandextras

Reference may be made to the Data sheet on page 2 and to the Relationships sheet.

STUDENT MARGIN

1   The following velocity–time graph represents the motion of a car travelling in a straight line.

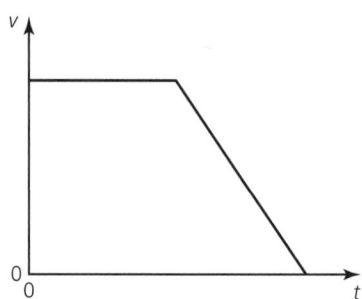

Which of the following displacement–time graphs represent the same motion?

A

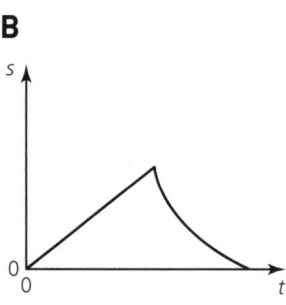

B

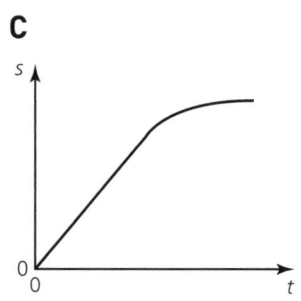

C

D

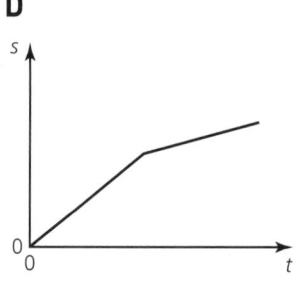

E

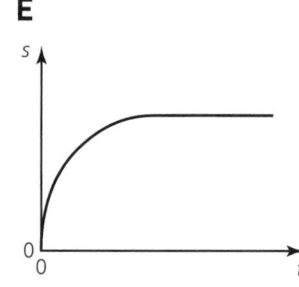

CAS
ODU 1.2
ODU 1.3

HTP
Pages 1–2

2 An object is accelerating at $5.0\,\mathrm{m\,s^{-2}}$. This means that the

- **A** distance travelled by the object increases by 5 metres every second
- **B** displacement of the object increases by 5 metres every second
- **C** speed of the object is $5\,\mathrm{m\,s^{-1}}$ every second
- **D** velocity of the object is $5\,\mathrm{m\,s^{-1}}$ every second
- **E** velocity of the object increases by $5\,\mathrm{m\,s^{-1}}$ every second.

CAS
ODU 1.1

HTP
Page 3

3 A vehicle is travelling in a straight line. Graphs of velocity and acceleration against time are shown below. Which pair of graphs could represent the motion of the vehicle?

A

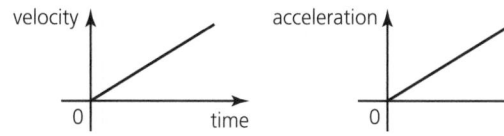

B

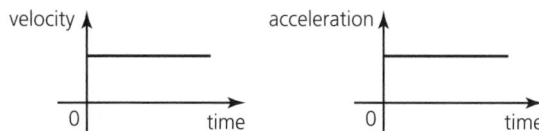

C

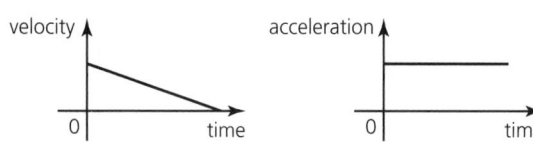

CAS
ODU 1.2
ODU 1.3

HTP
Pages 1–2

D

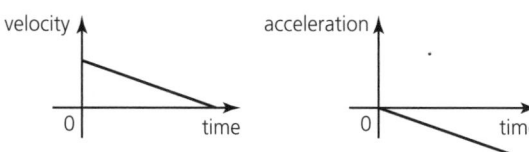

E

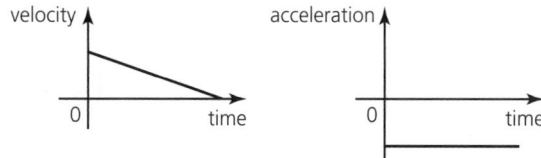

4 A model helicopter flies with constant velocity at constant height. Which diagram represents the forces acting on the helicopter?

A

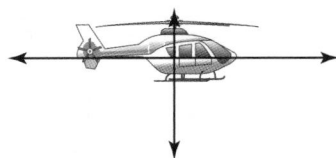

B

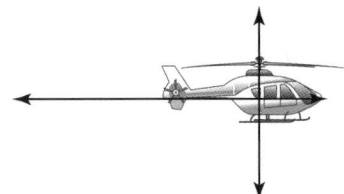

C

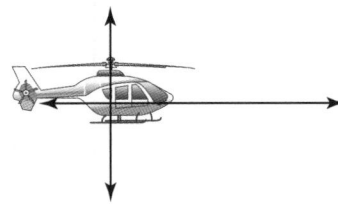

D

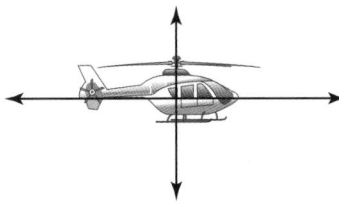

E

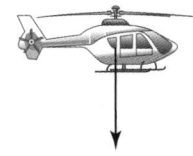

CAS
ODU 2.1

HTP
Page 10

5 An object of mass m is at rest on a slope.

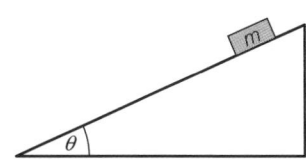

Which of the following pairs correctly shows the components of weight acting down and normal to the slope?

	Component down the slope	Component normal to the slope
A	$mg \tan \theta$	$mg \cos \theta$
B	$mg \sin \theta$	$mg \tan \theta$
C	$mg \sin \theta$	$mg \cos \theta$
D	$mg \cos \theta$	$mg \sin \theta$
E	$mg \cos \theta$	$mg \tan \theta$

CAS
ODU 2.6
ODU 2.8

HTP
Page 15

6 Two trolleys collide and stick together as shown. Initially, trolley A is moving at $0{\cdot}60\,\mathrm{m\,s^{-1}}$. It collides with and sticks to a stationary trolley, B. The trolleys move off together as shown, at $0{\cdot}30\,\mathrm{m\,s^{-1}}$.

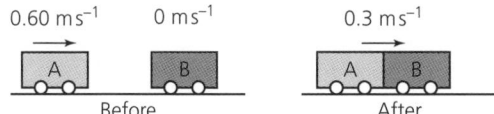

How do the masses of the trolleys compare?

A Trolley A has two times the mass of Trolley B.

B Trolley B has two times the mass of Trolley A.

C Trolley A has the same mass as Trolley B.

D Trolley A has four times the mass of Trolley B.

E Trolley B has four times the mass of Trolley A.

CAS
ODU 3.1

HTP
Pages 21–23

7 A satellite orbits a planet at a distance of $3{\cdot}0 \times 10^{7}\,\mathrm{m}$ from the centre of the planet. The mass of the satellite is $1{\cdot}8 \times 10^{4}\,\mathrm{kg}$. The mass of the planet is $4{\cdot}2 \times 10^{24}\,\mathrm{kg}$. The gravitational force acting on the satellite due to the planet is

A $8{\cdot}4 \times 10^{13}\,\mathrm{N}$

B $1{\cdot}7 \times 10^{11}\,\mathrm{N}$

C $5{\cdot}6 \times 10^{3}\,\mathrm{N}$

D $1{\cdot}7 \times 10^{3}\,\mathrm{N}$

E $8{\cdot}4 \times 10^{-3}\,\mathrm{N}$.

CAS
ODU 4.4

HTP
Pages 33–34

8   The graph shows how the energy emitted per second from the surface of a hot object varies with the wavelength, λ, of the emitted radiation at different temperatures.

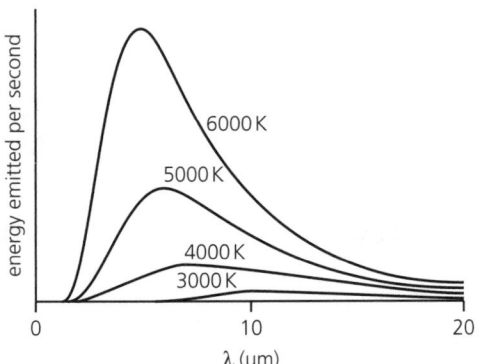

A student makes the following statements based on the information shown in the graph.

I   As the temperature of the object increases, the total energy emitted per second increases.

II   As the temperature of the object decreases, the peak wavelength of the emitted radiation increases.

III   The frequency of the emitted radiation steadily increases as the emitted energy per second decreases.

Which of the statements is/are correct?

A   I only

B   II only

C   III only

D   I and II only

E   II and III only

CAS
ODU 6.10

HTP
Page 46

9   Which of the following lists the particles in order of size from smallest to largest?

A   helium nucleus; electron; proton

B   helium nucleus; proton; electron

C   proton; helium nucleus; electron

D   electron; helium nucleus, proton

E   electron; proton; helium nucleus

CAS
P&W 1.1

HTP
Page 50

10 Radioactive beta decay gave the first evidence of the existence of the neutrino because

    A   the charge of the emitted particle is not constant

    B   the kinetic energy of the emitted particle is not constant

    C   the mass of the emitted particle is not constant

    D   the spin of the emitted particle is not constant

    E   the size of the emitted particle is not constant.

CAS
P&W 1.7

HTP
Page 51

11 Which of the following lists the charge on the particles correctly for the electric field patterns shown below:

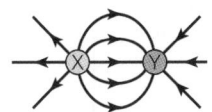 

	Charge X	Charge Y	Charge Z
A	positive	negative	negative
B	positive	negative	positive
C	negative	positive	negative
D	positive	positive	negative
E	negative	negative	positive

CAS
P&W 2.2

HTP
Page 54

12 The definition of the volt is

    A   the work done moving unit charge between two points

    B   the work done moving unit charge outside the electric field

    C   half the energy stored per unit charge in a capacitor

    D   the square root of energy divided by capacitance

    E   half the square root of energy divided by capacitance.

CAS
P&W 2.4

HTP
Page 56

13 A proton enters a magnetic field as shown in the diagram.

```
        X  X  X  X
  ⊕→ v   X  X  X  X
  +     X  X  X  X
        X  X  X  X
```

Which of the following describes the effect of the field on the proton's velocity vector?

    A   The magnitude of the velocity vector increases.

    B   The magnitude of the velocity vector decreases.

    C   The direction of the velocity vector changes towards the top of the field.

    D   The direction of the velocity vector changes towards the bottom of the field.

    E   The direction of the velocity vector changes to move out of the page.

CAS
P&W 2.7

HTP
Page 59

14 What is meant when two wave sources are described as coherent?

   A   The path difference between the two sources is constant.

   B   The irradiance of the two sources is constant.

   C   The amplitude of the two sources is fixed.

   D   The frequency difference between the two sources is constant.

   E   The phase difference between the two sources is constant.

CAS
P&W 5.2

HTP
Page 72

15 For the ray diagram below, which is the correct definition of refractive index, n?

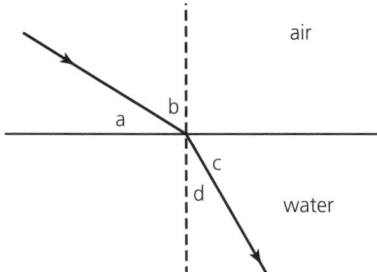

   A $n = \dfrac{\sin a}{\sin c}$

   B $n = \dfrac{\sin a}{\sin d}$

   C $n = \dfrac{\sin b}{\sin c}$

   D $n = \dfrac{\sin b}{\sin d}$

   E $n = \dfrac{1}{\sin a}$

CAS
P&W 6.1

HTP
Pages 80–81

16 The irradiance of a point source is measured at a particular distance from the source and found to be $54\,W\,m^{-2}$. What value would be measured at three times the distance from the source?

   A $54\,W\,m^{-2}$

   B $18\,W\,m^{-2}$

   C $12\,W\,m^{-2}$

   D $6{\cdot}0\,W\,m^{-2}$

   E $4{\cdot}5\,W\,m^{-2}$

CAS
P&W 7.1

HTP
Pages 91–92

17 The peak voltage of a source is measured to be $10{\cdot}0\,V$. What is the r.m.s. voltage value for this source?

   A $14{\cdot}1\,V$

   B $10{\cdot}0\,V$

   C $7{\cdot}07\,V$

   D $5{\cdot}0\,V$

   E $2{\cdot}23\,V$

CAS
E&E 1.2

HTP
Page 102

18 A 2000 μF capacitor is completely charged when the voltage across the plates is 4·5 V. How much energy is stored in the capacitor when it is fully charged?

A $4·05 \times 10^{-2}$ J

B $2·03 \times 10^{-2}$ J

C $1·01 \times 10^{-2}$ J

D $9·00 \times 10^{-3}$ J

E $4·50 \times 10^{-3}$ J

CAS
E&E 4.2

HTP
Page 110

19 Which of the following correctly describes the conduction and valence bands of an insulator?

A The conduction band overlaps the valence band.

B The conduction band is very close to the valence band.

C The conduction band is very far from the valence band.

D The conduction band is lower energy than the valence band.

E The conduction band is the same energy as the valence band.

CAS
E&E 5.2
E&E 5.4

HTP
Page123

20 A p-n junction is formed by joining two pieces of semiconductor. In the depletion region of the junction, which of the following statements are true?

A The majority of charge carriers in the depletion region are electrons.

B The majority of charge carriers in the depletion region are holes.

C The concentration of charge carriers in the depletion region is greater than in the p or n semiconductor.

D The concentration of charge carriers in the depletion region is lower than in the p or n semiconductor.

E The concentration of charge carriers in the depletion region is the same as in the p or n semiconductor.

CAS
E&E 5.7

HTP
P 125–126

[End of Section 1]

[Now attempt the questions in Section 2]

Section 2

MARKS

STUDENT MARGIN

1   Hillend is Europe's longest dry ski run with an overall piste length of 400 m, total vertical drop of 110 m and average slope angle of 16°.

A skier of total mass 70 kg ascends the slope using the ski-tow and then completes a run down the slope.

a)   The velocity–time graph of the first part of the uphill, ski-tow journey is shown.

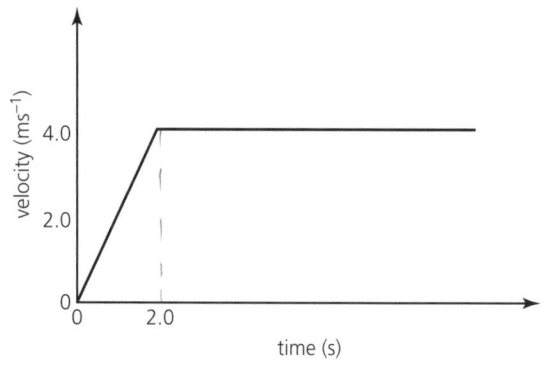

CAS
ODU 1.2
ODU 1.3
ODU 2.1

HTP
Pages 1–2

STUDENT
MARKS | MARGIN

(i) Calculate the resultant force experienced by the skier during the first 2·0 seconds of the ascent.

Space for working and answer

3

CAS
ODU 1.2
ODU 1.3
ODU 2.1

HTP
Pages 1–2

(ii) Determine the resultant force experienced by the skier after the first 2·0 seconds of the ascent.

Space for working and answer

1

CAS
ODU 1.2
ODU 1.3
ODU 2.1

HTP
Pages 1–2

b) Calculate the maximum kinetic energy of the skier as she arrives at the bottom of the slope.

Space for working and answer

3

CAS
ODU 2.10
ODU 2.11

HTP
Pages 9–10

c) The actual velocity of the skier at the bottom of the slope is determined to be 20·0 m s⁻¹. Calculate the average frictional force over the 400 m descent.

Space for working and answer

3

CAS
ODU 2.10
ODU 2.11

HTP
Pages 9–10

2 A car, mass 1500 kg, is towing a caravan of mass 1000 kg. The car accelerates uniformly from rest to a velocity of $22 \cdot 0 \, \text{m s}^{-1}$ in $12 \cdot 0$ seconds.

a) Show that the acceleration of the car and caravan is $1 \cdot 83 \, \text{m s}^{-2}$.

Space for working and answer

b) Calculate the magnitude of the accelerating force provided by the car engine.

Space for working and answer

c) Calculate the magnitude of the tension force in the tow bar connecting the car and caravan.

Space for working and answer

MARKS

3 A student is investigating the physics of snooker. Using light gates and a computer she determines the velocity of the white cue ball and the yellow ball that it hits. On a particular shot, the white hits the yellow and they both move off in the same direction along the same line as the original path of the white ball.

Her results are shown below:

	Velocity before strike (m s⁻¹)	Velocity after strike (m s⁻¹)
white ball	3·80	0·51
yellow ball	0·00	3·49

Mass of white ball: 0·17 kg
Mass of yellow ball: 0·16 kg

a) Show that momentum is conserved in the collision between the white and yellow balls.

Space for working and answer

3

CAS
ODU 3.1

HTP
Pages 20–23

b) State whether the collision elastic or inelastic. You must justify your answer.

Space for working and answer

3

CAS
ODU 3.2

HTP
Page 24

She now adjusts the experiment to measure the contact time between the cue and the white ball. The ball speed after being struck is 4·15 m s⁻¹. The contact time is measured as 0·35 ms.

c) Calculate the average force applied by the cue to the ball as it is struck.

Space for working and answer

3

CAS
ODU 3.7

HTP
Pages 25–26

4 Satellite navigation systems involve a network of satellites orbiting the Earth. Typical orbit altitudes are 20 200 km with an orbit period of 12 hours. The radius of the Earth is 6371 km and its mass is $5 \cdot 97 \times 10^{24}$ kg.

a) Calculate the magnitude of the velocity of a satellite in this network.

Space for working and answer

4

CAS
ODU 4.1
ODU 4.2

HTP
Pages 1–3

b) Calculate the magnitude of the gravitational force acting on a satellite of mass 250 kg in this network.

Space for working and answer

4

CAS
ODU 4.4

HTP
Pages 33–34

c) Explain why the magnitude of the satellite velocity is constant despite the unbalanced gravitational force acting on the satellite.

Space for working and answer

1

CAS
ODU 4.3

HTP
Page 33

STUDENT
MARKS   MARGIN

5 Muons are fundamental particles which are a constituent part of the solar radiation incident on the Earth. These muons travel at around 98% of the speed of light (0·98*c*).

For a stationary observer on Earth, calculate how many seconds pass on their clock for each second experienced by the muon.

Space for working and answer

3

CAS
ODU 5.3

HTP
Page 38

STUDENT
MARKS   MARGIN

6 Students observe an ambulance as it drives past them on the street. The ambulance is travelling at $28{\cdot}0\,\text{m s}^{-1}$ and emits a siren with a highest tone of $440\,\text{Hz}$ and lowest tone of $420\,\text{Hz}$. The speed of sound in air is $340\,\text{m s}^{-1}$.

a) Calculate the lowest frequency note heard by the student as the ambulance approaches.

3

Space for working and answer

CAS
ODU 6.1
ODU 6.2

HTP
Page 42

As the ambulance passes by, the student notes that the siren appears to change in frequency.

b) State what change in frequency is observed by the student.

1

Space for working and answer

CAS
ODU 6.1
ODU 6.2

HTP
Page 42

c) Calculate the highest frequency note heard by the student as the ambulance moves away.

3

Space for working and answer

CAS
ODU 6.1
ODU 6.2

HTP
Page 42

MARKS **STUDENT MARGIN**

7 Hadron matter particles are made up from fundamental particles called quarks. Hadrons may be classed as one of two types: baryons or mesons.

a) State how many quarks make up a baryon.

1

b) State how many quarks make up a meson.

1

c) Explain why, in general, mesons have a shorter lifetime than baryons.

2

CAS
P&W 1.5

HTP
Page 52

8 The following equation shows a nuclear reaction

$$^{235}_{92}U + ^{1}_{0}n \rightarrow ^{93}_{37}Rb + ^{141}_{55}Cs + 2^{1}_{0}n$$

Particle	Mass (kg)
^{235}U	$390{\cdot}173 \times 10^{-27}$
^{93}Rb	$154{\cdot}248 \times 10^{-27}$
^{141}Cs	$233{\cdot}927 \times 10^{-27}$
^{1}n	$1{\cdot}675 \times 10^{-27}$

a) State what type of nuclear reaction is shown.

1

CAS
P&W 3.1

HTP
Page 64

b) Explain why this type of reaction releases energy.

2

CAS
P&W 3.1
HTP
Page 65

c) Calculate the amount of energy released by the reaction shown.

Space for working and answer

4

CAS
P&W 3.1

HTP
Pages 65–66

d) A 30 MW nuclear power station is designed to use this reaction to generate electricity. Calculate the minimum number of reactions per second required to meet this demand.

Space for working and answer

4

CAS
P&W 3.1

HTP
Page 65–66

STUDENT
MARKS   MARGIN

9   The graph below shows the emitted electron kinetic energy versus incident light frequency results for a series of photoelectric effect experiments using three different metals (A, B and C).

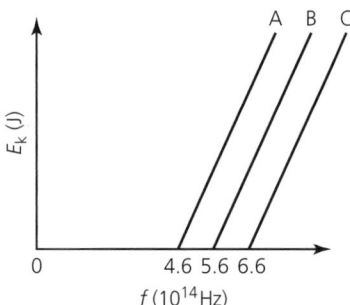

CAS
P&W 4.3
P&W 4.4

HTP
Page 90

a) Explain why the graph for each metal intersects the frequency axis at a different point.

2

b) Explain why the graph for each metal has the same gradient.

2

CAS
P&W 4.3
P&W 4.4

HTP
Page 91

c) Calculate the wavelength of the minimum frequency of light which causes electrons to be emitted for metal A.

4

Space for working and answer

CAS
P&W 4.3
P&W 4.4

HTP
Page 91

d) Estimate the colour of light associated with the minimum frequency of light which causes electrons to be emitted for metal A.

1

CAS
P&W 4.3
P&W 4.4

HTP
Page 91

10 The experiment below shows the interference pattern produced when a 1 mW green laser light, 550 nm, is incident on a diffraction grating with 300 lines per mm.

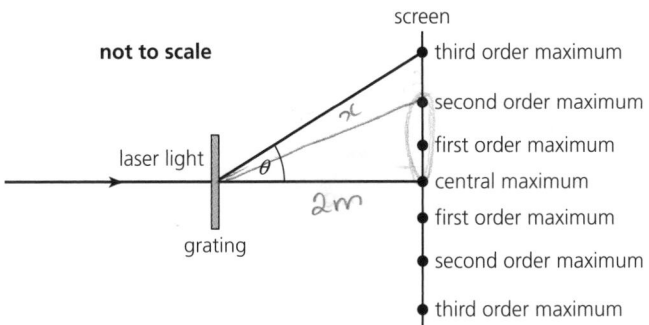

a) Explain why this experiment produces a series of equally spaced, bright green spots separated by dark regions on the screen.

3

CAS
P&W 5.4
P&W 5.5
P&W 5.6

HTP
Page 75

b) Calculate the distance from the central maximum to the second maximum observed on a screen 2·0 m from the grating.

Space for working and answer

4

CAS
P&W 5.4
P&W 5.5
P&W 5.6

HTP
Page 76

STUDENT
MARKS   MARGIN

c) The green laser is now replaced with a red laser source of the same power. Describe what changes would be observed to the pattern viewed on the screen. You must explain your answer.

3

CAS
P&W 5.4
P&W 5.5
P&W 5.6

HTP
Page 77

11 Diamond has a relatively high refractive index of 2·42 which affects its critical angle and causes its 'sparkle' when illuminated with light.

a) State what is meant by critical angle.

1

CAS
P&W 6.5

HTP
Page 84

b) Calculate the critical angle for diamond.

3

Space for working and answer

CAS
P&W 6.5

HTP
Page 85

12 The diagram below shows a model of part of the atomic electron energy levels for a particular element.

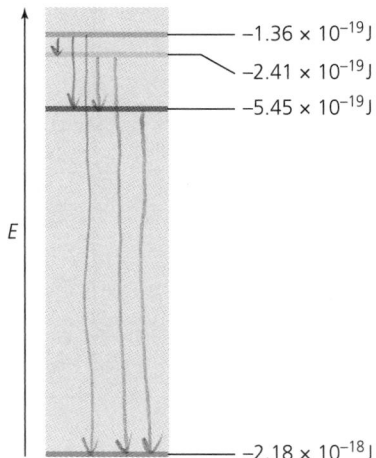

-1.36×10^{-19} J
-2.41×10^{-19} J
-5.45×10^{-19} J

E

-2.18×10^{-18} J

a) State how many possible electron energy level transitions are possible for this model.

1

b) Calculate the largest wavelength of light emitted by electrons in this model.

4

Space for working and answer

CAS

P&W 7.5
P&W 7.6
P&W 7.7
P&W 8.1
P&W 8.2

HTP
Page 95

CAS

P&W 7.5
P&W 7.6
P&W 7.7
P&W 8.1
P&W 8.2

HTP
Pages 96–97

13 The diagram below shows an oscilloscope trace for an a.c. electrical source.

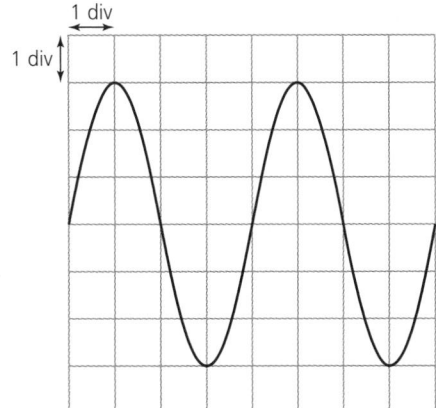

The time-base is set at 4·0 ms/div and the Y-gain is set at 50 V/div.

a) Calculate the frequency of this source.

Space for working and answer

b) Calculate the voltage rating for this source.

Space for working and answer

STUDENT
MARKS   MARGIN

14 The following circuit is used to measure the relationship between terminal potential difference and current in the load resistor in order to determine the e.m.f. and internal resistance of the battery.

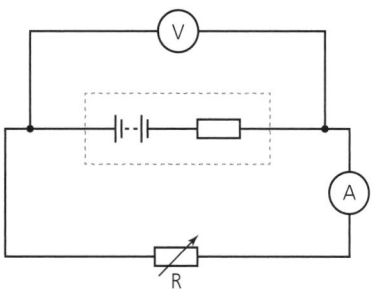

a) Explain what is meant by the terms **terminal potential difference** and **e.m.f.**

2

CAS
E&E 3.1
E&E 3.2

HTP
Page 106

The graph of the relationship between terminal potential difference and current obtained is shown below.

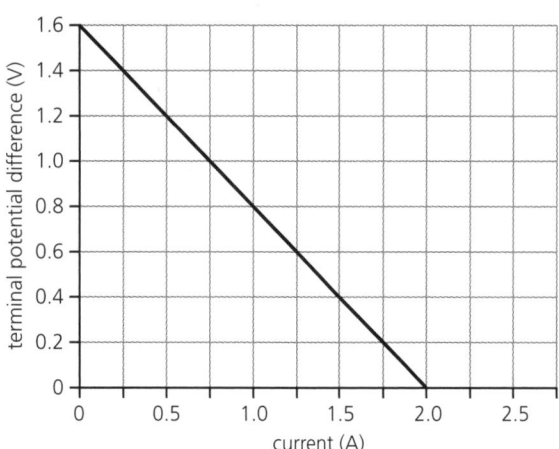

b) Use the graph to determine the e.m.f. of the supply.

1

CAS
E&E 3.1
E&E 3.2

HTP
P 108–109

c) Use the graph to determine the internal resistance of the supply.

Space for working and answer

4

CAS
E&E 3.1
E&E 3.2

HTP
P 108–109

15 The charge on a capacitor is measured using a coulomb meter.
The results are shown below:
1·03 nC, 1·04 nC, 1·01 nC, 1·06 nC, 1·08 nC

a) Calculate the mean value of the charge stored on
the capacitor.

Space for working and answer

b) Calculate the random uncertainty in the mean value of the
charge stored on the capacitor.

Space for working and answer

END OF PRACTICE PAPER A]

Higher
Physics

Data sheet

Common physical quantities

Quantity	Symbol	Value	Quantity	Symbol	Value
Speed of light in vacuum	c	3.00×10^8 m s^{-1}	Planck's constant	h	6.63×10^{-34} J s
Magnitude of the charge on an electron	e	1.60×10^{-19} C	Mass of electron	m_e	9.11×10^{-31} kg
Universal Constant of Gravitation	G	6.67×10^{-11} m^3 kg^{-1} s^{-2}	Mass of neutron	m_n	1.675×10^{-27} kg
Gravitational acceleration on Earth	g	9.8 m s^{-2}	Mass of proton	m_p	1.673×10^{-27} kg
Hubble's constant	H_0	2.3×10^{-18} s^{-1}			

Refractive indices

The refractive indices refer to sodium light of wavelength 589 nm and to substances at a temperature of 273 K.

Substance	Refractive index	Substance	Refractive index
Diamond	2·42	Water	1·33
Crown glass	1·50	Air	1·00

Spectral lines

Element	Wavelength/nm	Colour	Element	Wavelength/nm	Colour
Hydrogen	656	Red	Cadmium	644	Red
	486	Blue-green		509	Green
	434	Blue-violet		480	Blue
	410	Violet			
	397	Ultraviolet			
	389	Ultraviolet			

		Lasers	
Element	Wavelength/nm	Colour
Carbon dioxide	9550 ⎱ 10590 ⎰	Infrared
Helium-neon	633	Red

Sodium 589 Yellow

Properties of selected materials

Substance	Density/kg m^{-3}	Melting Point/K	Boiling Point/K
Aluminium	2.70×10^3	933	2623
Copper	8.96×10^3	1357	2853
Ice	9.20×10^2	273	. . . .
Sea Water	1.02×10^3	264	377
Water	1.00×10^3	273	373
Air	1·29	. . . .	. . . .
Hydrogen	9.0×10^{-2}	14	20

The gas densities refer to a temperature of 273 K and a pressure of 1.01×10^5 Pa.

Duration – 2 hours and 30 minutes

Total marks – 130

SECTION 1 – 20 marks

Attempt ALL questions.

SECTION 2 – 110 marks

Attempt ALL questions.

Reference may be made to the Data sheet on page 32 and to the Relationships sheet.

Care should be taken to give an appropriate number of significant figures in the final answers to calculations.

Write your answers clearly in the spaces provided in this paper. Any rough work must be written in this paper. You should score through your rough work when you have written your final copy.

Use **blue** or **black** ink.

B

Section 1

SECTION 1 – 20 MARKS

Attempt ALL questions – instructions/answer grid available at www.hoddereducation.co.uk/updatesandextras

Reference may be made to the Data sheet on page 32 and to the Relationships sheet.

STUDENT MARGIN

1. A ball has a potential energy of 1·5 J when raised. It is dropped and hits the ground at $2\,\text{m}\,\text{s}^{-1}$. Assuming no energy losses, the mass of the ball is

   A   0·15 kg

   B   0·375 kg

   C   0·75 kg

   D   1·50 kg

   E   3·00 kg.

   CAS
   ODU 2.11

   HTP
   Page 16

2. A block of mass 5·00 kg slides down a slope at an angle of 40°. Identify the correct component of weight acting parallel to the slope and acting normal to the slope from the table below.

	Parallel	*Normal*
A	41·1 N	37·5 N
B	31·5 N	41·1 N
C	31·5 N	37·5 N
D	37·5 N	31·5 N
E	37·5 N	41·1 N

   CAS
   ODU 2.8

   HTP
   Page 15

3. Which of the following could you determine from a speed–time graph?

   A   Power

   B   Force

   C   Distance

   D   Displacement

   E   Momentum

   CAS
   ODU 1.2

   HTP
   Page 4

4. A person of mass m jumps vertically from rest to a height h. The jump to maximum height takes t seconds. What is the power developed by the person during the jump?

   A $mght$

   B mgt

   C $\dfrac{mgt}{t}$

   D $\dfrac{mgh}{t}$

   E $\dfrac{t}{mgh}$

   CAS
   ODU 2.10

   HTP
   Page 16

5 A stationary golf ball of mass 170 g is struck by a golf club.
The force–time graph is shown below. What is the velocity of the ball immediately after impact?

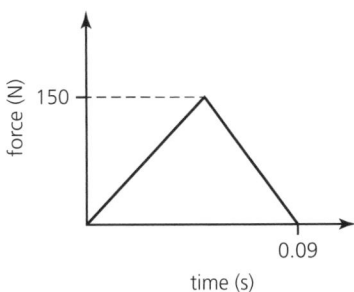

A $0 \cdot 06 \, \text{m s}^{-1}$

B $3 \cdot 6 \, \text{m s}^{-1}$

C $40 \, \text{m s}^{-1}$

D $79 \, \text{m s}^{-1}$

E $4900 \, \text{m s}^{-1}$

CAS
ODU 3.5

HTP
Page 26

6 A car is travelling towards a stationary student at $25 \, \text{m s}^{-1}$. It sounds its horn which operates at 750 Hz. What would the frequency heard by the observer be?

A   695 Hz

B   725 Hz

C   750 Hz

D   775 Hz

E   810 Hz

CAS
ODU 6.1

HTP
Page 15

7 A tow truck of mass 1200 kg pulls a car of mass 700 kg along a straight line with an acceleration of $2 \cdot 0 \, \text{m s}^{-2}$.
Assuming that the frictional forces acting on the car are negligible, the tension in the coupling is

A   500 N

B   1400 N

C   1900 N

D   2400 N

E   3800 N.

CAS
ODU 2.4

HTP
Page 10

8 A 4·0 kg box slides with a constant velocity down a slope.
The slope makes an angle of 30° with the horizontal.
What is the value of the force of friction acting on the box?

A   0 N

B   2·0 N

C   19·6 N

D   22·6 N

E   33·9 N

CAS
ODU 2.8

HTP
Page 15

9   Two loudspeakers are connected to the same signal generator. During an experiment, the first minimum from the central position is observed at point X as shown in the diagram below. What is the frequency of the sound wave?

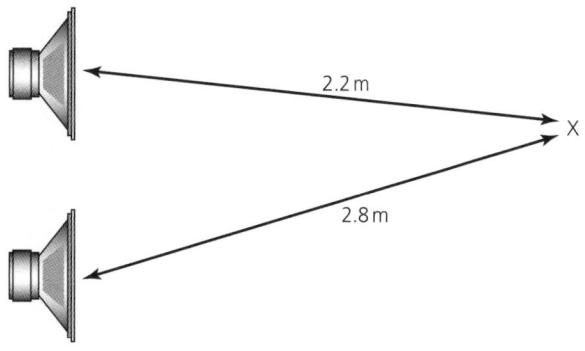

2.2 m

X

2.8 m

A   1·2 Hz
B   34 Hz
C   283 Hz
D   567 Hz
E   850 Hz

CAS
P&W 5.4

HTP
Page 73

10 A student is investigating the following light-sensing circuit. The resistance of the variable resistor is set to 6 kΩ.

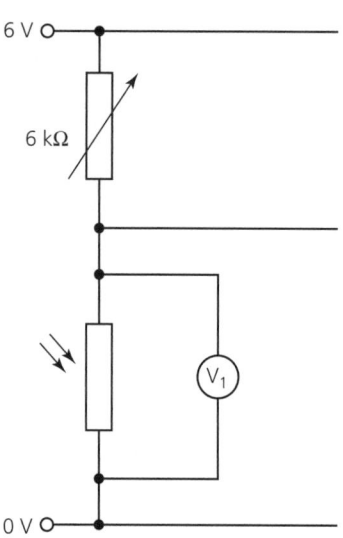

6 V

6 kΩ

V_1

0 V

At a certain light level the voltage V_1 is measured to be 1·50 V.
What is the current in the light dependent resistor at this light level?

A   0·25 mA
B   0·75 mA
C   1·00 mA
D   2·25 mA
E   3·00 mA

CAS
E&E 2.2

HTP
Page 105

11　An electron of charge $1 \cdot 6 \times 10^{-19}$ C and mass $9 \cdot 11 \times 10^{-31}$ kg accelerates through a potential difference of 3 kV. What is the energy gained by the electron due to the electric field?

A　$3 \cdot 0 \times 10^{-34}$ J

B　$2 \cdot 7 \times 10^{-27}$ J

C　$5 \cdot 3 \times 10^{-23}$ J

D　$4 \cdot 8 \times 10^{-16}$ J

E　$5 \cdot 7 \times 10^{-12}$ J

CAS
P&W 2.3

HTP
Page 56

12　One type of baryon consists of two up quarks and one down quark. The charge on a down quark is $-\frac{1}{3}$.

The charge on an up quark is $+\frac{2}{3}$.

Which row in the table shows the charge and type for this baryon?

	Charge	Type of baryon
A	+1	neutron
B	0	neutron
C	−1	neutron
D	−1	proton
E	+1	proton

CAS
P&W 1.5

HTP
Page 50

13　The following graph was obtained from an experiment on the photoelectric effect.

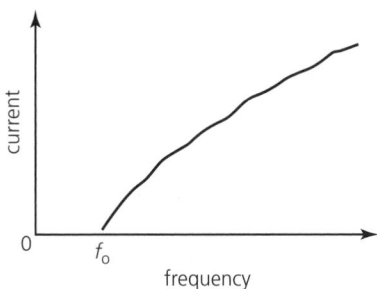

A student makes the following statements:

I　Below the threshold frequency, f_0, no electrons are ejected.

II　More electrons are ejected as the frequency of the photons increases.

III　Frequency, f_0, is the minimum frequency at which a neutron will be ejected.

Which of these statements is/are correct?

A　I only

B　II only

C　III only

D　I and II only

E　I, II and III

CAS
P&W 4.4

HTP
Page 89

14 In an experiment a student connects a length of copper wire to a 6 V supply. He notices that small plotting compasses change direction slightly when the circuit is connected. This is because

A the current in the copper attracts the North section of the compasses

B the charges in the copper become magnetic and attract the compasses

C the energy in the wire is dissipated as heat and interferes with the surrounding area

D the copper aligns itself with the magnetic field from the compasses

E the magnetic field produced by the charges moving in the copper wire affects the compasses.

CAS
P&W 2.6

HTP
Page 89

15 Light is shone from a ray box into a block of plastic as shown in the diagram below. Using the information provided in this diagram, find the refractive index of the plastic.

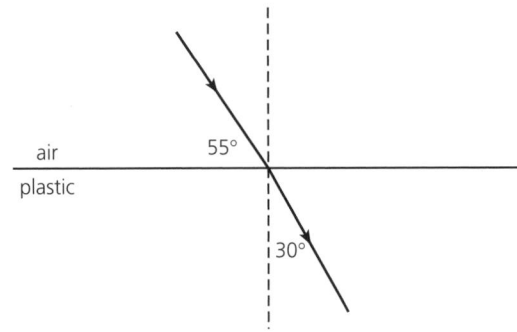

A 0·87

B 1·06

C 1·15

D 1·51

E 1·63

CAS
P&W 6.1

HTP
Page 80

16 Light from a filament lamp is passed through a glass prism and a spectrum is produced. The white light separates into its constituent frequencies which we observe as different colours.
How can this be explained?

A White light is a mixture of these frequencies.

B Different frequencies travel at different velocities and take longer to travel through the prism leading to separation.

C The white light combines while inside the glass to produce different frequencies upon leaving.

D Different frequencies have different refractive indices and travel at different angles as a result.

E The angles of the prism cause different frequencies to refract unequally.

CAS
P&W 6.4

HTP
Page 83

17 An alternating voltage is displayed on an oscilloscope screen.

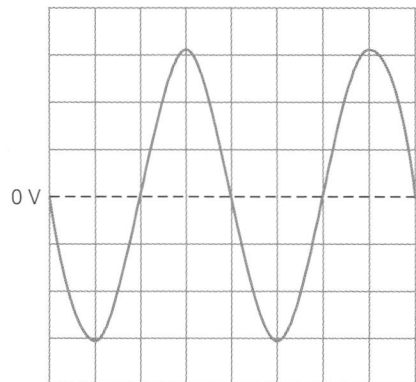

The timebase control is set to 8 ms/div.
The Y-gain control is set to 0·5 mV/div.
Which row in the table shows the correct frequency and peak voltage of the output signal?

	Frequency (Hz)	Peak voltage (V)
A	31·25	0·0015
B	31·25	1·5
C	62·5	667
D	125	1·5
E	125	0·0015

18 A student is given the following information about a capacitor: the energy stored when the capacitor is fully charged and the size of the capacitor. What relationship could the student use to calculate the charge held by the capacitor?

A $Q = \sqrt{2EC}$

B $Q = \sqrt{EC}$

C $Q = 2EC$

D $Q = \dfrac{\sqrt{EC}}{2}$

E $Q = 2EC^2$

19 A circuit is set up as shown.

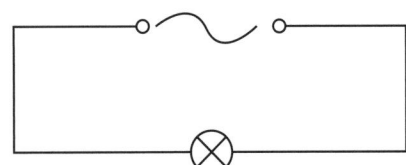

The r.m.s. voltage across the lamp is 9·0 V. The resistance of the lamp is 3·0 Ω. The peak current in the lamp is:

A 0·5 A

B 2·1 A

C 3·0 A

D 4·2 A

E 27 A.

CAS
E&E 1.2

HTP
Page 101

20 Light from the Sun was analysed and its spectra were observed. Close inspection found many small gaps in the spectra. They appear as fine, dark lines. They are caused by:

A gases in the outer layers of the Sun absorbing photons

B the central core of the Sun which does not emit light across the whole spectrum

C the dissipation of certain colours as the photons travel the long distance from the Sun to Earth

D the upper atmosphere of the Earth blocking certain colours

E the light from the Sun being refracted and diffracted on its journey to Earth.

CAS
P&W 8.3

HTP
Page 96

[End of Section 1]

[Now attempt the questions in Section 2]

Section 2

SECTION 2 – 110 marks

Attempt ALL questions.

Reference may be made to the Data sheet on page 32 and to the Relationships sheet.

Care should be taken to give an appropriate number of significant figures in the final answers to calculations.

Write your answers clearly in the spaces provided in this paper. Any rough work must be written in this paper. You should score through your rough work when you have written your final copy.

Use **blue** or **black** ink.

	MARKS	STUDENT MARGIN

1 A student is investigating the distance travelled by projectiles launched from a ramp. The angle of launch can be varied as can the height from which the projectile is released.

Projectile A has a mass of 1·25 kg and is raised through a height of 1·4 m.

a)

   (i)   Calculate the gain in potential energy of the projectile.

      Space for working and answer

3

CAS
ODU 3.1

HTP
Page 16

   (ii) Assuming no losses, calculate the velocity of the projectile during the horizontal section.

      Space for working and answer

4

CAS
ODU 2.10

HTP
Page 9

B

The section at C is used to change the angle of launch of the projectile and this is used in an experiment.

The velocity of the projectile as it left the launcher at an angle of 25° was measured at $4.5\,\mathrm{m\,s^{-1}}$.

b)

    (i) Calculate the horizontal component of the velocity at launch.

Space for working and answer

1

CAS
ODU 4.2

HTP
Page 13

    (ii) Calculate the vertical component of the velocity at launch.

Space for working and answer

1

CAS
ODU 4.2

HTP
Page 13

    (iii) Calculate the horizontal distance travelled by the projectile at this angle.

Space for working and answer

4

CAS
ODU 4.1

HTP
Page 31

    (iv) Sketch a graph showing how the horizontal velocity of the projectile varies with time until it hits the ground.

2

CAS
ODU 1.2

HTP
Page 5

Higher Physics

2   In satellite launches multi-stage rockets are used to place the
satellites in orbit around the Earth. The first stage takes the
rocket to a certain height, it is jettisoned and the second stage
takes it further.
The details for an experimental prototype are:
Stage 1: Mass of engine and casing = 3550 kg

Mass of fuel   = 2740 kg

Thrust of engine   = 120 000 N

Stage 2: Mass of engine and casing = 1650 kg

Mass of fuel   = 2150 kg
Thrust of engine   = 105 000 N

a)   Calculate the mass of the rocket at take off.   1
Space for working and answer

CAS
ODU 2.2

b)   Calculate the initial acceleration of the rocket.   5

Space for working and answer

CAS
ODU 2.1

HTP
Page 11

After the first stage has finished firing, the rocket is travelling
at 1300 m s⁻¹. The second stage rocket ignites and fires for 25 seconds.

c)   Assuming the stages have separated by this point, calculate the
impulse applied to the second stage.   3

Space for working and answer

CAS
ODU 3.7

HTP
Page 25

STUDENT
MARKS   MARGIN

In an earlier test launch, the first stage did not detach but the second stage engine still managed to fire.

d) What difference would this have on the impulse given to the rocket?

1

CAS
ODU 3.7

HTP
Page 25

e) What difference would this make to the change in velocity of the rocket? You must justify your answer.

2

CAS
ODU 3.7

HTP
Page 25

3 When the NASA Moon missions were in operation, the command/service modules orbited the Moon at a height of 190 km above the surface. The modules had a mass of 28 400 kg.

The mass of the Moon is $7 \cdot 34 \times 10^{22}$ kg.

The radius of the Moon is $1 \cdot 74 \times 10^6$ m.

a) Calculate the gravitational force between the Moon and the command module.

Space for working and answer

5

CAS
ODU 4.4

HTP
Page 33

In a simulation, the NASA scientists considered what would happen if the command module rockets malfunctioned and reduced the orbital velocity to zero.

b) Explain what would happen to the command module under these conditions.

2

CAS
ODU 4.1

HTP
Page 33

4   In the 1970s many car manufacturers tried to make their vehicles very rigid and able to survive a small collision with little or no deformation. Steering wheels and dashboards were made of toughened steel and aluminium.

Using your knowledge of physics, explain how changes in motor vehicle design and construction have made cars safer for drivers and passengers.

3

CAS
ODU 3.2

MARKS STUDENT MARGIN

5 A theme park has a small train composed of an engine and three carriages. The mass of the engine and driver is 2750 kg and each carriage is 1450 kg.
The engine produces 6500 N of force when pulling the carriages.

a) Calculate the initial acceleration of the train.

Space for working and answer

4

CAS
ODU 2.4

HTP
Page 10

b) Calculate the tension in the coupling between the engine and the carriages as it moves off.

Space for working and answer

2

CAS
ODU 2.4

HTP
Page 10

c) When operating, the train has a top speed of $2.4\,m\,s^{-1}$.
During one run the final carriage was removed from the train. What effect would this have on the train's acceleration and top speed? You must justify your answer.

2

CAS
ODU 2.3

HTP
Page 11

B

6   A synchrotron is used to accelerate particles for scientific study. It uses a combination of electric and magnetic fields.

   a)   What is the purpose of the magnetic field?

   b)   What is the purpose of the electric field?

A proton, initially at rest, reaches an energy of 75 MeV.

   c)   Calculate the velocity of the proton at this energy.

   Space for working and answer

An improvement in the device claims it could double the energy of particles within it.

   d)   Explain what effect this improvement would have upon the velocity of the proton.

7 A cyclotron is used to accelerate protons as shown.

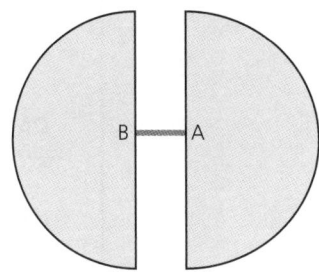

a) A proton at rest is accelerated across the gap from A to B at a voltage of 60 kV. Calculate the velocity of the proton at point B.

Space for working and answer

b) Sketch an energy–time graph for the proton for the first four occasions it crosses the gap.

STUDENT
MARKS MARGIN

8 Both nuclear fusion and nuclear fission reactions can result in the release of energy.

a) Explain/describe what occurs in a fission reaction.

3

CAS
P&W 3.1

HTP
Page 64

b) Calculate the energy released in the following fusion reaction:

$^3_1H + ^3_1H \rightarrow ^4_2He + 2\,(^1_0n)$

4

Particle	Mass (kg)
^3_1H	$5{\cdot}00827 \times 10^{-27}$
^4_2He	$6{\cdot}64648 \times 10^{-27}$
^1_0n	$1{\cdot}67493 \times 10^{-27}$

Space for working and answer

CAS
P&W 3.1

HTP
Page 65

c) Why are fusion reactors for power generation seen by some as a better alternative to fission reactors?

2

CAS
P&W 3.1

HTP
Page 67

STUDENT
MARKS   MARGIN

9 A 12V lead/acid car battery is being used to test starter
motors prior to them being fitted to car engines.
Thick copper connecting leads from the battery are attached to the
motors and then they are switched on.
When not connected to the motors, the voltage across the battery
is found to be 12·3V. When connected, the current from the
battery is measured at 65A and the voltage across the
battery was 9·2V.

a) Calculate the internal resistance of the battery.   3

Space for working and answer

CAS
E&E 3.1

HTP
Page 106

When removing the leads from the motor, the technician
accidentally allowed the connecting clamps to glance off each other.
This led to a large spark being seen by the technician.

b) Suggest a reason why the spark was seen.   2

CAS
E&E 3.1

HTP
Page 106

c) Why are thick leads used during these tests?   2

CAS
E&E 3.1

HTP
Page 106

The same battery is used by the technician to charge a 220 mF capacitor and is connected in the circuit as shown.

12V

d) When could the technician determine that the capacitor has been fully charged?

2

CAS
E&E 4.2

HTP
Page 106

e) On another occasion the technician only has an ammeter for use. How could this be used to determine when the capacitor is fully charged?

2

CAS
E&E 4.2

HTP
Page 112

The capacitor is connected to a separate circuit with a component of resistance of 85 Ω.

f) Calculate the initial current as the capacitor discharges.

Space for working and answer

3

CAS
E&E 4.3

HTP
Page 112

This component is replaced with one of 225 Ω.

g) What effect would this have on the initial current and the time taken for the capacitor to discharge?

2

CAS
E&E 4.3

HTP
Page 112

10 A triangular glass prism of refractive index 1·4 is used in an experiment as shown.

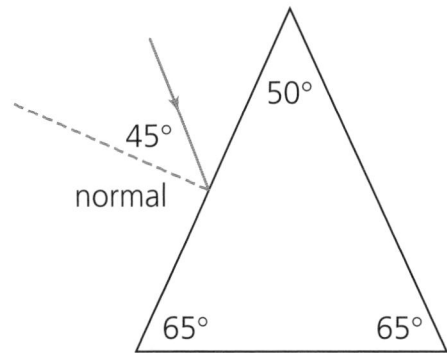

A ray of white light is directed at the prism as shown.
Complete the path the ray takes until it exits the prism.
(You must show all working/angles.)

8

CAS
P&W 6.1

HTP
Page 72

11 A laser is projected onto a diffraction grating as shown.
The light has a wavelength of 565 nm.
The spacing of the grating, $d = 3.5 \times 10^{-6}$ m.

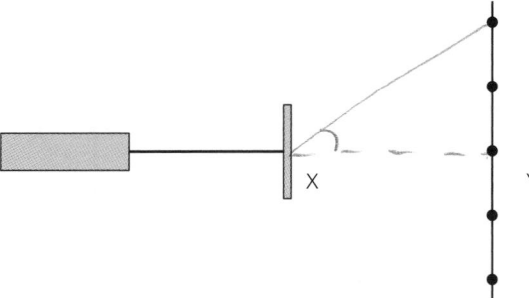

Bright spots are seen on the screen as shown.

a) Calculate the angle between the central and the second order maximum.

Space for working and answer

b) A light detector is moved between points X and Y.
Describe what it would register.

4

2

CAS
P&W 5.6

HTP
Page 76

CAS
P&W 5.6

HTP
Page 76

12 While studying distant galaxies, Hubble and others noted that all galaxies appear to be moving away from us. Furthermore it was found that distant galaxies are moving away from us more rapidly. Data such as these were obtained from clusters in various galaxies:

Distance (light years)	Velocity (km/s)
1.00×10^9	1.50×10^4
1.40×10^9	2.20×10^4
2.50×10^9	3.90×10^4

a) Convert the distances in this table to m. You can use 1 year as 365·25 days.

Space for working and answer

3

b) Convert the velocities to m s⁻¹.

Space for working and answer

2

c) Calculate a value for Hubble's constant from these data.

Space for working and answer

3

d) What possible value for the age of the Universe would this give?

Space for working and answer

2

[END OF PRACTICE PAPER B]

Higher
Physics

HODDER
GIBSON
LEARN MORE

Data sheet

Common physical quantities

Quantity	Symbol	Value	Quantity	Symbol	Value
Speed of light in vacuum	c	$3{\cdot}00 \times 10^8 \, \text{m s}^{-1}$	Planck's constant	h	$6{\cdot}63 \times 10^{-34} \, \text{J s}$
Magnitude of the charge on an electron	e	$1{\cdot}60 \times 10^{-19} \, \text{C}$	Mass of electron	m_e	$9{\cdot}11 \times 10^{-31} \, \text{kg}$
Universal Constant of Gravitation	G	$6{\cdot}67 \times 10^{-11} \, \text{m}^3 \, \text{kg}^{-1} \, \text{s}^{-2}$	Mass of neutron	m_n	$1{\cdot}675 \times 10^{-27} \, \text{kg}$
Gravitational acceleration on Earth	g	$9{\cdot}8 \, \text{m s}^{-2}$	Mass of proton	m_p	$1{\cdot}673 \times 10^{-27} \, \text{kg}$
Hubble's constant	H_0	$2{\cdot}3 \times 10^{-18} \, \text{s}^{-1}$			

Refractive indices

The refractive indices refer to sodium light of wavelength 589 nm and to substances at a temperature of 273 K.

Substance	Refractive index	Substance	Refractive index
Diamond	2·42	Water	1·33
Crown glass	1·50	Air	1·00

Spectral lines

Element	Wavelength/nm	Colour	Element	Wavelength/nm	Colour
Hydrogen	656	Red	Cadmium	644	Red
	486	Blue-green		509	Green
	434	Blue-violet		480	Blue
	410	Violet			
	397	Ultraviolet			
	389	Ultraviolet			

			Lasers		
			Element	Wavelength/nm	Colour
Sodium	589	Yellow	Carbon dioxide	9550 } 10590 }	Infrared
			Helium-neon	633	Red

Properties of selected materials

Substance	Density/kg m^{-3}	Melting Point/K	Boiling Point/K
Aluminium	$2{\cdot}70 \times 10^3$	933	2623
Copper	$8{\cdot}96 \times 10^3$	1357	2853
Ice	$9{\cdot}20 \times 10^2$	273	. . . .
Sea Water	$1{\cdot}02 \times 10^3$	264	377
Water	$1{\cdot}00 \times 10^3$	273	373
Air	1·29	. . . .	. . . .
Hydrogen	$9{\cdot}0 \times 10^{-2}$	14	20

The gas densities refer to a temperature of 273 K and a pressure of $1{\cdot}01 \times 10^5 \, \text{Pa}$.

Duration – 2 hours and 30 minutes

Total marks – 130

SECTION 1 – 20 marks

Attempt ALL questions.

SECTION 2 – 110 marks

Attempt ALL questions.

Reference may be made to the Data sheet on page 58 and to the Relationships sheet.

Care should be taken to give an appropriate number of significant figures in the final answers to calculations.

Write your answers clearly in the spaces provided in this paper. Any rough work must be written in this paper. You should score through your rough work when you have written your final copy.

Use **blue** or **black** ink.

C

Section 1

SECTION 1 – 20 MARKS

Attempt ALL questions – instructions/answer grid available at www.hoddereducation.co.uk/updatesandextras

Reference may be made to the Data sheet on page 58 and to the Relationships sheet.

STUDENT MARGIN

1   The following graph shows the velocity–time relationship for a ball dropped from a height at time $t = 0$.

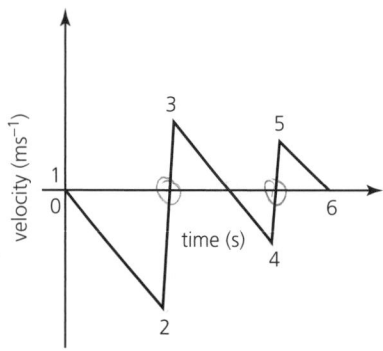

Between which points is the ball in contact with the ground?

A   1 and 2

B   3 and 4

C   5 and 6

D   2 and 3 & 4 and 5

E   3 and 4 & 5 and 6

CAS
ODU 1.4

HTP
Page 6

2   The following graph shows the speed–time relationship for a parachutist's journey from the aircraft to the ground.

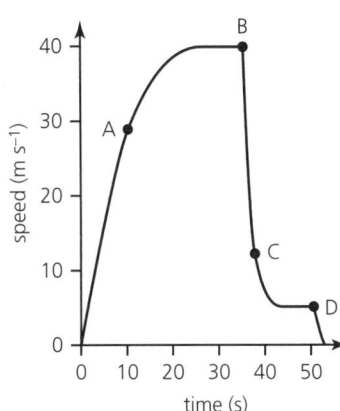

Which statement describes the forces acting on the parachutist between points B and C?

A   Weight force is greater than upthrust.

B   Weight force is less than upthrust.

C   Weight force is equal to upthrust.

D   Weight force is zero.

E   Upthrust is zero.

CAS
ODU 2.5

HTP
Page 12

3   The forces acting on an object are shown in the diagram below.

Which of the following is the resultant force vector acting on the object?

A   8·6 N at 036

B   8·6 N at 054

C   12 N at 036

D   12 N at 054

E   5 N at 036

CAS
ODU 2.7

HTP
Pages 13–14

4   A 3·5 kg mass is raised through a height of 2·4 m in 30 seconds using an electric winch. What is the minimum power output of the electric winch motor?

A   8·4 J

B   8·4 W

C   2·7 J

D   2·7 W

E   105 W

CAS
ODU 2.11

HTP
Page 16

5 A missile explodes into two fragments X and Y. One piece (X) moves off with a velocity of $48\,m\,s^{-1}$; the other (Y) moves off in the opposite direction with a velocity of $24\,m\,s^{-1}$. Which one of the following statements is true?

   A   X has the same mass as Y.

   B   X has half the mass of Y.

   C   X has twice the mass of Y.

   D   X has three times the mass of Y.

   E   X has a third the mass of Y.

CAS
ODU 3.3

HTP
Page 24

6 A mass is projected off a cliff. Which of the following statements is true?

   I   The horizontal acceleration is zero.

   II   The horizontal velocity is constant.

   III   The vertical acceleration is zero.

   A   I only

   B   II only

   C   III only

   D   I and II only

   E   I and III only

CAS
ODU 4.2

HTP
Pages 30–32

7 A spacecraft is moving towards the Earth at $2.0 \times 10^8\,m\,s^{-1}$ as a forward-facing laser shines towards the Earth. The speed of the light received is measured by a stationary observer on the Earth's surface. What is the speed of light measured by the observer?

   A $1.0 \times 10^8\,m\,s^{-1}$

   B $2.0 \times 10^8\,m\,s^{-1}$

   C $3.0 \times 10^8\,m\,s^{-1}$

   D $4.0 \times 10^8\,m\,s^{-1}$

   E $5.0 \times 10^8\,m\,s^{-1}$

CAS
ODU 5.1

HTP
Page 38

8 A distant galaxy is moving away from the Earth and the light it emits is analysed to determine the wavelength of its spectral lines. A particular line is measured to have $\lambda = 700\,nm$. The same line emitted from a gas sample on Earth has $\lambda = 630\,nm$. The red-shift of the distant galaxy is

   A   0.1

   B   0.11

   C   0.9

   D   1.11

   E   5.89.

CAS
ODU 6.3

HTP
Pages 42–43

9 We can estimate the mass of a galaxy by:

   A   the peak irradiance wavelength emitted by the stars within it

   B   the recession velocity of the galaxy

   C   the distance between the Earth and the galaxy

   D   the red-shift of the light emitted by the stars within it

   E   the orbital speed of stars within it.

CAS
ODU 6.7

HTP
Page 45

10 Which of the following statements is/are true?

  I   Quarks are fermions.
  II   Leptons are fermions.
  III Force-mediating particles are bosons.
  A   I only
  B   II only
  C   III only
  D   I and II only
  E   I, II and III

CAS
P&W 1.4–1.6

HTP
Pages 50–52

11 Electromagnetic radiation of frequency 9.5×10^{14} Hz is incident on a section of metal. The work function of the metal is 5.2×10^{-19} J.
The maximum kinetic energy of a photoelectron released from the surface is:

  A 1.1×10^{-19} J
  B 2.5×10^{-19} J
  C 4.3×10^{-19} J
  D 5.2×10^{-19} J
  E 6.3×10^{-19} J.

CAS
P&W 4.1

HTP
Page 89

12 A student describes an electric field with the following statements.

  I   A charge in an electric field will experience a balanced force.
  II   A charge in the field will move downwards.
  III When an electric field is applied to a conductor, the free charges in the conductor move.

Which statement(s) is/are correct?

  A   I and II
  B   I, II and III
  C   I only
  D   II only
  E   III only

CAS
P&W 2.3

13 In a photodiode, which of the following happens when a photon enters an n-type semiconductor?

  A   The photon is converted to an electron and aids conduction.
  B   The photon is absorbed by an electron.
  C   The photon replaces an electron.
  D   The energy of the photon enables an electron to move from the valence to the conduction band.
  E   The energy of the photon is emitted as light.

CAS
E&E 5.5

HTP
Page 54

14 A student measures the irradiance of light from a point source at various distances and notes the following results:

Irradiance (W m^{-2})	Distance (m)
45·0	0·05
5·2	0·15
1·8	0·25
0·2	0·75

The irradiance of the light at a distance of 1·1 m from the source is:

A 0·15 W m^{-2}

B 0·97 W m^{-2}

C 0·050 W m^{-2}

D 0·097 W m^{-2}

E 0·0097 W m^{-2}.

CAS
P&W 7.1

HTP
Page 91

15 Dark matter has been proposed as an unusual form of non-baryonic matter which is responsible for most of the matter in the Universe. The main evidence for its existence comes from

A the temperature of stars in distant galaxies

B the rate of rotation of galaxies

C the cosmic microwave background radiation

D stellar growth and formation

E particles found very shortly after the Big Bang.

CAS
ODU 6.8

HTP
Page 45

16 In an optics experiment a ray of light is seen to travel between two transparent materials as shown.

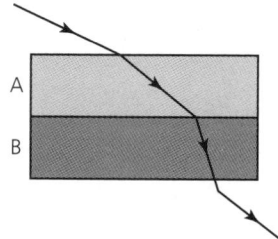

What can be said about light from this diagram?

A The frequency of the light in material A is greater than the frequency in air.

B The velocity of light in material B is greater than the velocity in material A.

C Material B has a greater refractive index than material A.

D Material A has a greater refractive index than material B.

E The wavelength of light in A and B is the same.

CAS
P&W 6.3

HTP
Page 80

17 The photon energies for three different radiations are as follows

Radiation 1: $2 \cdot 78 \times 10^{-19}$ J
Radiation 2: $5 \cdot 24 \times 10^{-19}$ J
Radiation 3: $6 \cdot 35 \times 10^{-19}$ J.
Which statement is correct?

A The wavelength of radiation 1 is longer than that of radiation 2.

B The wavelength of radiation 3 is longer than that of radiation 2.

C The frequency of radiation 1 is higher than that of radiation 2.

D The frequency of radiation 1 is higher than that of radiation 3.

E The frequency of radiation 2 is higher than that of radiation 3.

CAS
P&W 8.2

HTP
Page 90

18 Monochromatic light of wavelength λ passes through a grating and produces a pattern of bright maxima on a screen. The separation of lines is d and the grating is at a distance L from the screen. Which changes will produce an increase in the spacing of maxima on the screen?

A Increase L; increase d

B Increase λ; increase d

C Decrease L; decrease λ

D Increase L; decrease λ

E Increase λ; decrease d

CAS
P&W 5.6

HTP
Page 76

19 A $46\,\mu$F capacitor is connected to a $9\,$V d.c. supply. The supply is then increased to $15\,$V d.c. The gain in energy is

A $0 \cdot 21 \times 10^{-3}$ J

B $0 \cdot 35 \times 10^{-3}$ J

C $1 \cdot 9 \times 10^{-3}$ J

D $3 \cdot 3 \times 10^{-3}$ J

E $5 \cdot 2 \times 10^{-3}$ J.

CAS
E&E 4.2

HTP
Page 111

20 The resistivity of a wire is given by the relationship

$\rho = RA/l$

where:

R is the resistance of the wire

A is the cross-sectional area of the wire

l is the length of the wire.

The resistivity of a particular wire is $6 \cdot 2 \times 10^{-8}\,\Omega\,\mathrm{m}$.

The length of this wire is 65 m.

The wire has a circular cross section of radius 5 mm.

The resistance of the wire is

A $0 \cdot 0075\,\Omega$

B $0 \cdot 05\,\Omega$

C $0 \cdot 062\,\Omega$

D $0 \cdot 065\,\Omega$

E $0 \cdot 075\,\Omega$.

CAS
E&E

[End of Section 1]

[Now attempt the questions in Section 2]

Section 2

SECTION 2 – 110 marks

Attempt ALL questions.

Reference may be made to the Data sheet on page 58 of the question paper and to the Relationships sheet.

Care should be taken to give an appropriate number of significant figures in the final answers to calculations.

Write your answers clearly in the spaces provided in this paper. Any rough work must be written in this paper. You should score through your rough work when you have written your final copy.

Use **blue** or **black** ink.

MARKS   STUDENT MARGIN

1   A radio-controlled drone was being used to survey an area of land. It flew 175 m due North, then 225 m on a bearing of 60 West of North. It took 2 minutes and 20 seconds to complete this journey.

   a)

   (i)   Calculate the displacement of the drone during this flight.

   Space for working and answer

CAS
ODU 1.1

HTP
Pages 1–3

MARKS

(ii) Calculate the average velocity of the drone during this flight.

Space for working and answer

2

b) The drone then flew directly back to its starting point in a further 1 minute 50 seconds.

Calculate the average speed of the drone during the whole journey.

Space for working and answer

3

CAS
ODU 1.1

HTP
Page 1

2 A ball is dropped from a height of 1·75 m onto a laboratory floor.

a)

    (i) Calculate the time it takes to hit the ground.

Space for working and answer

    (ii) Calculate the velocity of the ball at the moment before it hits the ground.

Space for working and answer

The ball then rebounds to a height of 1·23 m.

b)

    (i) Calculate the velocity of the ball at the moment it leaves the ground.

Space for working and answer

    (ii) Calculate the total time the ball takes to return to the floor after the first rebound.

Space for working and answer

c) Use these data to draw a velocity–time graph for the ball from when it is dropped until it reaches the ground for the second time.

MARKS	STUDENT MARGIN
3	**CAS** ODU 1.4 **HTP** Page 3
3	**CAS** ODU 1.4 **HTP** Pages 5–6
3	**CAS** ODU 1.4 **HTP** Page 6
3	**CAS** ODU 1.4 **HTP** Page 6
3	**CAS** ODU 1.3 **HTP** Page 6

C

3 A tanker is being towed by two tug boats as shown in the diagram below.

The mass of the tanker is 2.84×10^6 kg. Each tug can exert a maximum force of 40.0 kN.

a) Calculate the magnitude of the resultant force applied by the combination of both tugs.

Space for working and answer

4

b) Calculate the direction of the resultant force applied by the combination of both tugs.

Space for working and answer

3

c) Calculate the maximum acceleration of the tanker as a result of the towing force provided by the combination of both tugs.

Space for working and answer

3

d) In reality, the acceleration of the tanker will be less than the maximum acceleration calculated in part c). Explain why the actual acceleration is less than predicted (assume the answer in part c) was calculated correctly).

1

4   The Moon orbits the Earth as shown in the diagram.

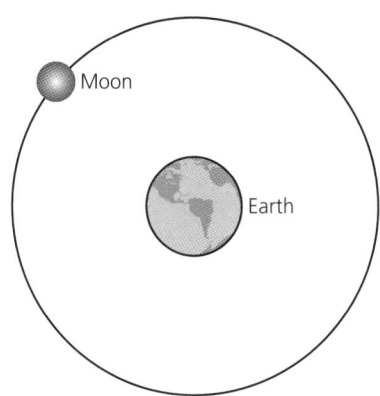

Data for the Moon–Earth orbit are as follows:

Mass of Moon (M_m): $7\cdot35 \times 10^{22}$ kg	Orbit distance (R): $3\cdot85 \times 10^5$ km
Mass of Earth (M_e): $5\cdot97 \times 10^{24}$ kg	Orbit period: $27\cdot32$ days

a)   Calculate the magnitude of the gravitational force between the Earth and the Moon.

Space for working and answer

b)   State the vector direction of the gravitational force acting on the Moon.

3

CAS
ODU 4.4
ODU 4.5

HTP
Pages 33–34

1

CAS
ODU 4.4
ODU 4.5

HTP
Pages 33–34

c) A spacecraft is travelling from the Earth to the Moon.
The resultant gravitational force acting on the spacecraft is a
vector combination of the force exerted by both the Earth and
the Moon. At a particular distance, r_m, from the Moon, the
resultant gravitational force will be zero.

Use the equation below to determine the value of r_m.

$$\sqrt{\frac{M_e}{M_m}} = \frac{R}{r_m} - 1$$

Space for working and answer

3

CAS
ODU 4.4
ODU 4.5

HTP
Pages 33–34

MARKS | STUDENT MARGIN

5 When Hubble observed distant galaxies, it was noted that all galaxies appeared to be moving away from our own galaxy. It was found that distant galaxies were moving away from us at a greater velocity than galaxies that are closer to us.

Using your knowledge of physics, comment on these observations.

3

CAS
ODU 6.4
ODU 6.5

HTP
Page 43

6 A star emits radiation across a range of wavelengths. The peak wavelength, λ_{peak}, is related to the surface temperature of the star by the formula

$$T = \frac{2 \cdot 898 \times 10^{-3}}{\lambda_{peak}}.$$

A scientist reported that our Sun has a λ_{peak} of $5 \cdot 05 \times 10^{-9}\,\text{m}$.

a) Calculate a value for the surface temperature of our Sun.

Space for working and answer

3

CAS
ODU 6.10

HTP
Page 46

b)

(i) The average temperature of space in our region is generally around $2 \cdot 0\,\text{K}$.

Calculate the peak wavelength of radiation associated with this temperature.

Space for working and answer

3

CAS
ODU 6.10

HTP
Page 46

(ii) What name is given to this radiation? Explain why this supports the Big Bang theory of our Universe's existence.

3

CAS
ODU 6.12

HTP
Page 47

7 The kinetic energy distribution of the beta particles emitted by a ^{14}C radioactive source is shown below:

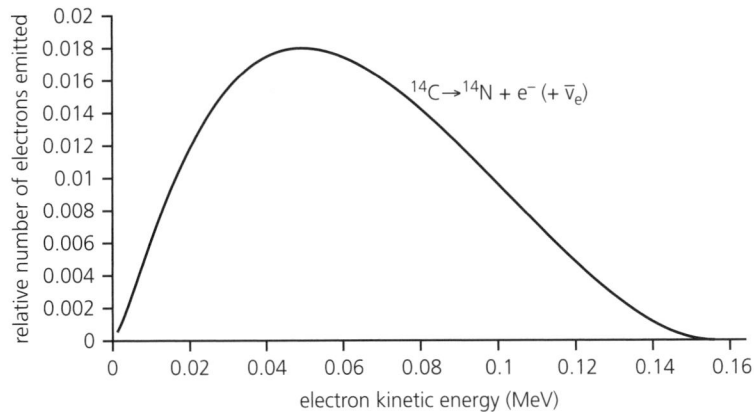

$^{14}C \rightarrow ^{14}N + e^- (+ \bar{v}_e)$

Note that $1 \cdot 0 \, MeV = 1 \cdot 6 \times 10^{-13} \, J$.

a) Explain why energy distributions such as these were used as the first evidence for the existence of the neutrino.

b) Calculate the most common velocity of the beta particles emitted in this reaction.

Space for working and answer

2

CAS
P&W 1.7

HTP
Page 51

4

CAS
P&W 1.7

STUDENT
MARKS   MARGIN

8 The diagram below shows equipment used to investigate the photoelectric effect.

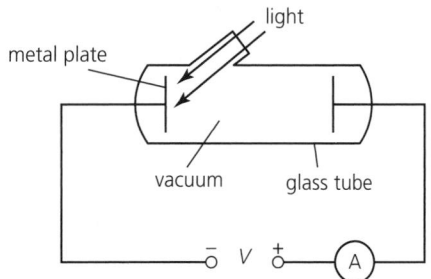

a) When green light is used to illuminate the target, no current flows. What colour of visible light may be used to cause a current to be detected? You must explain your answer.

3

CAS
P&W 4.1
P&W 4.2
P&W 4.3
P&W 4.4

HTP
Page 89

b) The work function for the metal plate is $2{\cdot}8 \times 10^{-19}$ J. Calculate the minimum frequency of light which would cause a current to be detected.

Space for working and answer

3

CAS
P&W 4.1
P&W 4.2
P&W 4.3
P&W 4.4

HTP
Page 91

9 Microwaves are passed through two slits (A and B) in a metal plate as shown in the diagram below. The slit separation is 0·045 m.

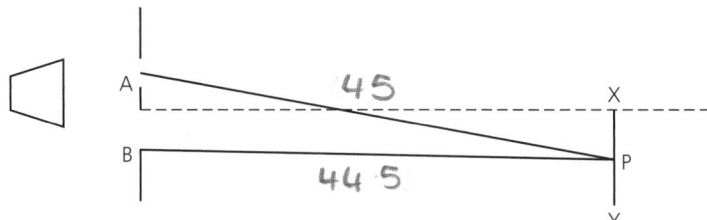

A detector is moved along a straight line from X to Y as shown and detects the first minimum at point P. Distance AP is 45·0 cm and distance BP is 44·5 cm.

a) Calculate the wavelength of the microwaves.

Space for working and answer

2

b) Calculate the angle at which the first maximum would be detected.

Space for working and answer

4

10 Ion propulsion engines are efficient at propelling satellites through space. In a simplified example, xenon ions are accelerated from one end of an engine to the exhaust. The ions being ejected in one direction causes a force to be applied on the spacecraft in the opposite direction.

The spacecraft has a mass of 450 kg. The mass of a xenon ion is $2 \cdot 8 \times 10^{-25}$ kg, its charge is $1 \cdot 6 \times 10^{-19}$ C and it is accelerated through a voltage of $2 \cdot 5$ kV.

a) Calculate the gain in energy of a xenon ion as it travels through the electric field.

Space for working and answer

3

CAS
P&W 2.5

HTP
Page 56

b) Assuming the ion is initially at rest, calculate the speed of the ion as it leaves the engine.

Space for working and answer

3

CAS
P&W 2.5

HTP
Pages 56–61

c) During a firing, $2 \cdot 0 \times 10^{-4}$ kg of xenon ions are ejected in 90 seconds.

Calculate the average thrust this would generate.

Space for working and answer

3

CAS
P&W 2.5

HTP
Pages 25–26

STUDENT
MARKS   MARGIN

11 A student investigates how irradiance, *I*, varies with distance, *d*, from a small lamp. The following apparatus is set up in a darkened laboratory.

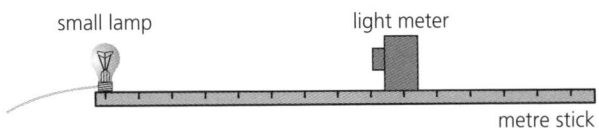

small lamp   light meter

metre stick

CAS
P&W 7.1
P&W 7.2
P&W 7.3

HTP
Page 92

a) State what is meant by irradiance.

1

b) A graph of the student's data collected in this experiment is shown below.

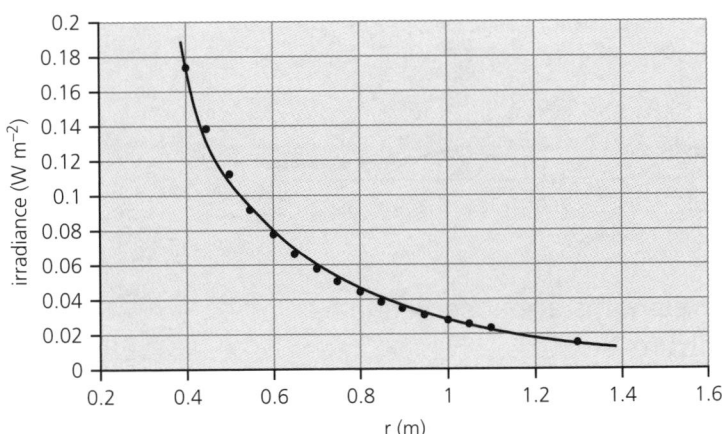

What further processing of the raw data is necessary in order to show a relationship of direct proportion between irradiance and distance?

2

CAS
P&W 7.1
P&W 7.2
P&W 7.3

HTP
Pages 93–94

c) Explain why the experiment is carried out in a darkened laboratory.

1

CAS
P&W 7.1
P&W 7.3

HTP
Page 132

12 Fraunhofer lines are any of the dark (absorption) lines in the spectrum of the Sun or other star. A typical spectrum of the light emitted by a star is shown below. The wavelengths labelled C, F, G and H lines correspond to specific wavelengths in the hydrogen atom emission.

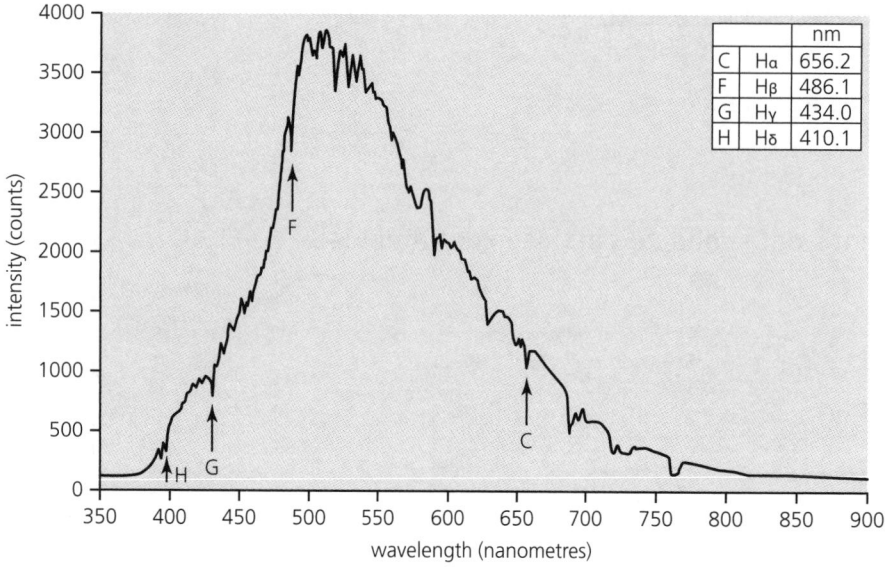

		nm
C	Hα	656.2
F	Hβ	486.1
G	Hγ	434.0
H	Hδ	410.1

a) Explain why only specific wavelengths are observed to be missing from the star's spectrum.

2

CAS
P&W 7.4

HTP
Page 96

b) For the hydrogen spectrum lines shown, calculate the minimum atomic electron energy transition associated with photons of these wavelengths.

4

CAS
P&W 7.4

HTP
Page 97

13 A student is investigating batteries for use in a circuit.
One battery is rated 9 V. The student inserts it into a circuit
as shown.

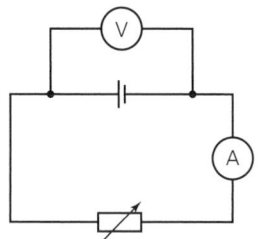

The student sets the resistance and measures the voltage and
current. The resistance is altered and a number of readings are taken.
These are shown in the table.

Voltage (V)	Current (A)
5·8	2·9
7·2	1·8
7·8	1·3
8·0	1·0

a) Use these results to draw a graph of voltage against current.

4

CAS
E&E 3.2

HTP
Page 108

b) Using this graph, determine:
   (i) the e.m.f. of the battery

1

CAS
E&E 3.2

HTP
Pages
108–109

   (ii) the internal resistance of the battery.

3

CAS
E&E 3.2

HTP
Pages
108–109

STUDENT
MARKS MARGIN

14 A student is investigating the following circuit

12.0V
(A)

4.40 kΩ   0–10.0 kΩ

a) 1.3uΩ.

   (i) Initially the ammeter shows a reading of 1·22 mA.
       Calculate the resistance of the variable resistor.   3

       Space for working and answer

CAS
E&E 2.1

HTP
Page 103

   (ii) Calculate the voltage across the variable resistor.   3

       Space for working and answer

CAS
E&E 2.1

HTP
Page 103

b) A 1·30 kΩ resistor is connected in parallel to the 4·40 kΩ resistor.
   (i) Calculate the total resistance of this pair of resistors
       connected in parallel.   3

       Space for working and answer

CAS
E&E 2.1

HTP
Pages
103–105

   (ii) What effect will this change have on the voltage across
       the variable resistor? You must justify your answer.   2

       Space for working and answer

CAS
E&E 2.1

HTP
Pages
103–105

[END OF PRACTICE PAPER C]

Higher
Physics

Practice Paper A

Section 1

Question	Answer	Mark	Commentary with hints and tips
1	C	1	The area under a velocity–time graph is the displacement for that part of the journey. Initially constant velocity means displacement increases at a constant rate. The constant rate of decrease in velocity means the rate of increase in displacement is positive but decreasing.
2	E	1	The definition of acceleration is the rate of change of velocity. For a constant $5 \cdot 0\,\mathrm{m\,s^{-2}}$ acceleration, velocity increases at a rate of $5 \cdot 0\,\mathrm{m\,s^{-1}}$ every second.
3	E	1	The gradient of a velocity–time graph is the acceleration of the object. Each v–t has a constant gradient, so the value of acceleration must be a constant (horizontal line). The v–t gradient is negative.
4	D	1	Newton's first law means that constant or zero velocity implies balanced forces in the velocity vector direction. Constant horizontal and vertical velocity requires balanced forces in both the horizontal and vertical.
5	C	1	Resolving the vertical weight force vector ($W = mg$) into components parallel and perpendicular to the slope gives answer C.
6	C	1	Conservation of total linear momentum ($p = mv$) requires that the total momentum before and after the collision is the same. The velocity has halved so the total mass has doubled.
7	C	1	Using $F = G\dfrac{m_1 m_2}{r^2}$ where $m_1 = 4 \cdot 2 \times 10^{24}$, $m_2 = 1 \cdot 8 \times 10^4$ and $r = 3 \cdot 0 \times 10^7$ gives answer C. Forgetting to square r is a very common error.
8	D	1	Reading the graph shows that ■ area under the curve (total energy emitted) increases with temperature increase ■ the peak wavelength value decreases (moves right) as temperature decreases ■ larger values of emitted energy occur for smaller values of wavelength λ. Therefore, I and II are correct.
9	E	1	Electron $< 10^{-18}\,\mathrm{m}$; Proton $< 10^{-15}\,\mathrm{m}$; Helium nucleus (two protons + two neutrons) > proton size
10	B	1	The emitted electron has a range of kinetic energy but the nuclear decay is a quantum change and so should always have the same energy. This must mean another particle is emitted (the neutrino).
11	B	1	Field lines show the direction of force experienced by a unit positive test charge. Like charges repel.
12	A	1	The definition of the volt comes directly from $E_\mathrm{w} = QV$, so $V = \dfrac{E_\mathrm{w}}{Q}$

Question	Answer	Mark	Commentary with hints and tips
13	C	1	The left-hand rule for positive charges in magnetic fields predicts the proton will be deflected upwards. The velocity vector direction changes but the velocity vector magnitude stays the same.
14	E	1	Coherent sources have a constant phase difference, i.e. the same frequency and wave speed in the medium.
15	D	1	Refractive index is always >1. Angles are measured between the ray and the normal.
16	D	1	Irradiance to distance is an inverse square relationship. Therefore, increasing the distance by a factor of 3 reduces the irradiance by a factor of 9 (3^2).
17	C	1	$V_{pk} = \sqrt{2}V_{rms}$ therefore $V_{rms} = \dfrac{V_{pk}}{\sqrt{2}}$
18	B	1	$E = \dfrac{1}{2}CV^2$; a common error is to forget to square the voltage
19	C	1	Insulators do not conduct because there are no charge carriers in the conduction band and the energy gap between the valence and conduction bands is too large for the charge carriers to move into the conduction bands.
20	D	1	In the depletion region of the p-n junction, the concentration of free charge carriers is reduced by the combination of electrons and holes on the formation of the junction.

Section 2

Question			Expected response	Maximum mark	Commentary with hints and tips
1	a)	(i)	From the graph, $a = \dfrac{4\cdot0}{2\cdot0} = 2\cdot0\,\mathrm{m\,s^{-2}}$ $F = ma$ $F = 70 \times 2 = 140\,\mathrm{N}$	3	The slope of a v–t graph is the acceleration of the object. The resultant (unbalanced) force gives rise to the acceleration of the object.
		(ii)	From the graph, $a = 0\,\mathrm{m\,s^{-2}}$ Therefore $F = 0\,\mathrm{N}$	1	The slope of a v–t graph is the acceleration of the object. A horizontal line has zero gradient.
	b)		$E_k = E_p$ $E_k = mgh$ $E_k = 70 \times 9\cdot8 \times 110$ $E_k = 7\cdot546 \times 10^4\,\mathrm{J}$ $E_k = 7\cdot5 \times 10^4\,\mathrm{J}$	1 1 1	Conservation of energy means that the maximum kinetic energy at the bottom of the slope is the total potential energy at the top of the slope. Poorest significant figure in the question is 2 s.f., so answer to 2 s.f.
	c)		$E_k = \dfrac{1}{2}mv^2$ $E_k = \dfrac{1}{2} \times 70 \times 20^2$ $E_k = 1\cdot4 \times 10^4\,\mathrm{J}$ $E_w = F.s$ $(7\cdot5 \times 10^4 - 1\cdot4 \times 10^4) = F \times 400$ $F = 1\cdot5 \times 10^2\,\mathrm{N}$	3	Some of the original potential energy is dissipated by work against friction. The difference between the maximum and actual kinetic energy gives the value of work against friction. Poorest significant figure in the question is 2 s.f., so answer to 2 s.f.
2	a)		$v = u + at$ $22\cdot0 = 0 + a \times 12\cdot0$ $a = \dfrac{22\cdot0}{12\cdot0}$ $a = 1\cdot83\,\mathrm{m\,s^{-2}}$	2	In 'show' questions, you must write down the equation, substitute the correct numbers for the symbols and show an equation which leads to the answer. The final line should show the value and units for the answer.
	b)		$F = ma$ $F = (1500 + 1000) \times 1\cdot83$ $F = 4575\,\mathrm{N}$ $F = 4\cdot58 \times 10^3\,\mathrm{N}$	3	The car engine accelerates both the car and caravan, so both masses must be used. Poorest significant figure in the question is 3 s.f., so answer to 3 s.f.
	c)		$F = ma$ $F = (1000) \times 1\cdot83$ $F = 1830$ $F = 1\cdot83 \times 10^3\,\mathrm{N}$	3	The tension in the tow bracket provides the acceleration force for the caravan, so just the mass of the caravan is used. Poorest significant figure in the question is 3 s.f., so answer to 3 s.f.

	Question		Expected response	Maximum mark	Commentary with hints and tips
3	a)		$p_{before} = m_1u_1 + m_2u_2$ $p_{before} = 0.17 \times 3.8 + 0.16 \times 0.0$ $p_{before} = 0.65\,kg\,m\,s^{-1}$ $p_{after} = m_1v_1 + m_2v_2$ $p_{after} = 0.17 \times 0.51 + 0.16 \times 3.49$ $p_{after} = 0.65\,kg\,m\,s^{-1}$	3	Momentum conservation means that the total linear momentum before and after collision is the same. Note that this is true when using the correct number of significant figures (i.e. 2 s.f.).
	b)		Before: $E_k = \frac{1}{2}mv^2$ $E_k = \frac{1}{2} \times 0.17 \times 3.8^2$ $E_k = 1.23\,J$ After: $E_k = \frac{1}{2}mv^2$ $E_k = \frac{1}{2} \times 0.17 \times 0.51^2 + \frac{1}{2} \times 0.16 \times 3.49^2$ $E_k = 0.997\,J$ The collision is inelastic as the kinetic energy is not conserved.	3	Kinetic energy conservation determines whether the collision is elastic or not.
	c)		Impulse $= F \times t = (mv - mu)$ $F \times 0.35 \times 10^{-3} = 0.17 \times 4.15$ $F = 2.02 \times 10^3\,N$ $F = 2.0 \times 10^3\,N$	3	Impulse is given by both $F \times t$ AND $(mv - mu)$. The cue ball starts at rest, therefore $u = 0.0\,m\,s^{-1}$. The time in the question is in milliseconds ($\times 10^{-3}\,s$). Poorest significant figure in the question is 2 s.f., so answer to 2 s.f.
4	a)		$s = 2\pi r$ $s = 2\pi(20\,200 + 6371) \times 10^3$ $s = vt$ $v = \frac{2\pi(20\,200 + 6371) \times 10^2}{12 \times 60 \times 60}$ $v = 3.8646 \times 10^3\,m\,s^{-1}$ $v = 3.9 \times 10^3\,m\,s^{-1}$	1 1 1 1	The distance travelled by the satellite is the circumference of a circular orbit. The time for the journey is the period of the orbit. The radius of orbit = the altitude + the radius of the Earth. The distances in the question are in km. Poorest significant figure in the question is 2 s.f., so answer to 2 s.f.
	b)		$r = (20\,200 + 6371) \times 10^3\,m$ $F = \frac{Gm_1m_2}{r^2}$ $F = \frac{6.67 \times 10^{-11} \times 5.97 \times 10^{24} \times 250}{(26\,571 \times 10^3)^2}$ $F = 141.0\,N$ $F = 1.41 \times 10^2\,N$	1 1 1 1	The radius of orbit = the altitude + the radius of the Earth. The distances in the question are in km. Poorest significant figure in the question is 3 s.f., so answer to 3 s.f.

	Question		Expected response	Maximum mark	Commentary with hints and tips
		c)	Acceleration is a change of velocity vector. The velocity vector direction is constantly changing while the magnitude is a constant value.	1	
5			$t' = \dfrac{t}{\sqrt{1 - \left(\dfrac{v}{c}\right)^2}}$ $t' = \dfrac{1}{\sqrt{1 - (0.98)^2}}$ $t' = 5.02519\,s$ $t' = 5.0\,s$	1 1 1	The velocity is given as $0.98c$, therefore $\dfrac{v}{c} = 0.98$. The question asks for the muon time for each second of stationary observer, so $t = 1\,s$. Poorest significant figure in the question is 2 s.f., so answer to 2 s.f.
6	a)		$f_o = f_s\left(\dfrac{v}{v - v_s}\right)$ $f_o = 420\left(\dfrac{340}{340 - 28.0}\right)$ $f_o = 457.69\,Hz$ $f_o = 458\,Hz$	1 1 1	The ambulance is approaching (separation is reducing) so the equation has $v - v_s$ in the denominator. Poorest significant figure in the question is 3 s.f., so answer to 3 s.f.
	b)		The frequency appears to change from higher to lower as the ambulance moves past the observer.	1	
	c)		$f_o = f_s\left(\dfrac{v}{v + v_s}\right)$ $f_o = 440\left(\dfrac{340}{340 + 28.0}\right)$ $f_o = 406.52\,Hz$ $f_o = 407\,Hz$	1 1 1	The ambulance is moving away (separation is increasing) so the equation has $v + v_s$ in the denominator. Poorest significant figure in the question is 3 s.f., so answer to 3 s.f.
7	a)		Three	1	
	b)		Two	1	
	c)		Mesons are made up of an antiquark and a quark. When they collide, they annihilate and emit photons of radiation. Baryons are either all antimatter or all matter quarks and are therefore more stable.	1 1	

	Question		Expected response	Maximum mark	Commentary with hints and tips
8	a)		Induced nuclear fission	1	
	b)		There is a mass difference between the reactants and products.	1	
			This mass is converted to energy (using $E = mc^2$).	1	
	c)		Mass before: $390 \cdot 173 + 1 \cdot 675$ $= 391 \cdot 848$	1	It is much easier to have all masses in the same unit (e.g. $\times 10^{-27}$ kg). Laying out the calculation as shown makes the arithmetic clear.
			Mass after: $154 \cdot 248 + 233 \cdot 927 +$ $3 \cdot 35 = 391 \cdot 525$	1	
			Mass difference $= 391 \cdot 848 -$ $391 \cdot 525$	1	
			$= 0 \cdot 323 \times 10^{-27}$ kg	1	
			$E = mc^2$		
			$E = 0 \cdot 323 \times 10^{-27} \times (3 \times 10^8)^2$		
			$E = 2 \cdot 907 \times 10^{-11}$ J		
	d)		$P = \dfrac{E}{t}$	4	The number of reactions per second (N) is given by $\dfrac{P}{E}$.
			$N = \dfrac{P}{E}$		Poorest significant figure in the question is 2 s.f., so answer to 2 s.f.
			$N = \dfrac{30 \times 10^6}{2 \cdot 907 \times 10^{-11}}$		
			$N = 1 \cdot 03188 \times 10^{18}$		
			$N = 1 \cdot 0 \times 10^{18}$		
9	a)		The work function (minimum energy needed to remove an electron from the metal surface) is given by hf_0. Work function is dependent on the metal structure and is therefore different for each metal.	1 1	$E_k = hf_0 + hf$ is the equation for photoelectric emission. Using $y = mx + c$ for any straight line gives the x-axis intercept as f_0.
	b)		The relationship between incident photon energy and frequency is $E = hf$. The gradient of each energy–frequency line must therefore be the same value (i.e. Planck's constant, h).	1 1	$E_k = hf_0 + hf$ is the equation for photoelectric emission. Using $y = mx + c$ for any straight line gives the gradient as h.
	c)		From graph, minimum frequency is $4 \cdot 6 \times 10^{14}$ Hz	1	Poorest significant figure in the question is 2 s.f., so answer to 2 s.f.
			$v = f\lambda$	1	
			$3 \times 10^8 = 4 \cdot 6 \times 10^{14} \times \lambda$	1	
			$\lambda = 6 \cdot 5217 \times 10^{-7}$ m	1	
			$\lambda = 6 \cdot 5 \times 10^{-7}$ m		
	d)		650 nm light is in the red range of the visible spectrum.	1	Spectral lines listed on the data sheet give example wavelengths and colours.

	Question		Expected response	Maximum mark	Commentary with hints and tips
10	a)		Laser light is separated into multiple coherent sources by the grating.	1	Answer must include:
			Light from these coherent sources travels different distances to reach the screen.	1	■ coherent sources
			When this path difference is an exact multiple of the light wavelength, the light from multiple sources interferes constructively to give a bright spot (all other path differences result in destructive interference).	1	■ path difference ■ condition for constructive interference.
	b)		$d = \dfrac{1 \times 10^{-3}}{300} = 3 \cdot 33 \times 10^{-6}\,\text{m}$ $m\lambda = d \sin \theta = d\dfrac{D}{L}$ $2 \times 550 \times 10^{-9} = 3 \cdot 33 \times 10^{-6} \times \dfrac{D}{2 \cdot 0}$ $D = 0 \cdot 66067\,\text{m}$ $D = 0 \cdot 66\,\text{m}$	1 1 1 1	300 lines per millimetre gives a line spacing of $\dfrac{1\,\text{mm}}{300}$ as shown. The geometry of the layout means that $\sin \theta = \tan \theta = \dfrac{D}{L}$, where L is the distance to the screen and D is the distance between the central maximum and the maximum being observed. Poorest significant figure in the question is 2 s.f., so answer to 2 s.f.
	c)		The wavelength of red light is larger than that of green light.	1	
			Given $m\lambda = d \sin \theta$, increasing λ while holding all other variables constant means that $\sin \theta$ and so θ increases, i.e. the pattern spacing increases.	1	
			The output power and irradiance are constant and so the brightness of the spots should remain constant.	1	
11	a)		As a wave moves from a more dense to a less dense medium, the critical angle is the minimum incident angle beyond which total internal reflection takes place.	1	
	b)		$\sin \theta_c = \dfrac{1}{n}$ $\sin \theta_c = \dfrac{1}{2 \cdot 42}$ $\theta_c = \sin^{-1}\left(\dfrac{1}{2 \cdot 42}\right)$ $\theta_c = 24 \cdot 407$ $\theta_c = 24 \cdot 4\,°$	1 1 1	Poorest significant figure in the question is 3 s.f., so answer to 3s.f.

	Question		Expected response	Maximum mark	Commentary with hints and tips
12	a)		6	1	There are six possible ways of moving between the atomic electron energy levels shown.
	b)		$E = E_3 - E_2 = (-1.36 - -2.41) \times 10^{-19}$ $E = 1.05 \times 10^{-19}$ J $E = hf$ $1.05 \times 10^{-19} = 6.63 \times 10^{-34} \times f$ $f = 1.5988 \times 10^{14}$ Hz $v = f\lambda$ $3 \times 10^8 = 1.5988 \times 10^{14} \times \lambda$ $\lambda = 1.876 \times 10^{-6}$ m $\lambda = 1.88 \times 10^{-6}$ m	1 1 1 1	The largest wavelength must have the smallest frequency. The smallest frequency is the smallest energy gap between levels. Poorest significant figure in the question is 3 s.f., so answer to 3 s.f.
13	a)		Period $T = 4 \times 4.0 \times 10^{-3}$ $T = 16 \times 10^{-3}$ s $f = \dfrac{1}{T}$ $f = \dfrac{1}{16 \times 10^{-3}}$ $f = 62.5$ Hz $f = 63$ Hz	1 1 1 1	Count the number of squares for one complete wave and use the time-base setting to calculate the time for one wave. Poorest significant figure in the question is 2 s.f., so answer to 2 s.f.
	b)		Peak voltage $V_{pk} = 3 \times 50$ $V_{pk} = 150$ V $V_{pk} = \sqrt{2}V_{rms}$ $150 = \sqrt{2}V_{rms}$ $V_{rms} = \dfrac{150}{\sqrt{2}}$ $V_{rms} = 106.066$ $V_{rms} = 110$ V	1 1 1 1	Count the number of squares for one complete wave and use the time-base setting to calculate the time for one wave. Poorest significant figure in the question is 2 s.f., so answer to 2 s.f.
14	a)		Terminal potential difference is the amount of energy per coulomb of charge delivered to the circuit components by an electrical source. E.m.f. is the amount of energy gained by each coulomb of charge as it passes through an electrical source.	1 1	These definitions (and any others in the course specification) should be learned as part of your revision.
	b)		1·6 V	1	The value of e.m.f. is the point at which the line intersects the voltage axis.

A

	Question		Expected response	Maximum mark	Commentary with hints and tips
	c)		$\text{Gradient} = \dfrac{(y_2 - y_1)}{(x_2 - x_1)}$ $\text{Gradient} = \dfrac{(1 \cdot 6 - 0 \cdot 4)}{(0 - 1 \cdot 5)}$ Gradient = $-0 \cdot 80$ So internal resistance, $r = 0 \cdot 80 \, \Omega$	1 1 1 1	Internal resistance is given by the gradient of the graph $V = -rI + E$ $y = mx + c$ so gradient $m = -r$
15	a)		Mean = sum/count Mean = $\dfrac{1 \cdot 03 + 1 \cdot 04 + 1 \cdot 01 + 1 \cdot 06 + 1 \cdot 08}{5}$ Mean = $1 \cdot 044$ Mean = $1 \cdot 04 \, \text{nC}$	1 1 1	
	b)		$\text{Random uncertainty} = \dfrac{\text{range}}{\text{number of values}}$ $= \dfrac{(1 \cdot 08 - 1 \cdot 01)}{5}$ $= 0 \cdot 014$ $= 0 \cdot 01 \, \text{nC}$	1 1 1	Uncertainty should only have 1 s.f.

Practice Paper B

Section 1

Question	Answer	Mark	Commentary with hints and tips
1	C	1	$E_p = E_k$; $1.5 = \frac{1}{2} \times m \times v^2$; $m = \frac{1.5 \times 2}{4} = \frac{3}{4} = 0.75\,\text{kg}$. Equate energies. Use 1.5 J to calculate mass.
2	C	1	Resolve the weight into components parallel and perpendicular: $Fd = m \times g \times \sin 40 = 31.5\,\text{N}$; $Fo = m \times g \times \cos 40 = 37.5\,\text{N}$
3	C	1	The area under a speed–time graph is the distance.
4	D	1	Power is $\dfrac{\text{energy}}{\text{time}}$. This leads to $P = \dfrac{E}{t} = \dfrac{(m \times g \times h)}{t}$
5	C	1	Calculate the area under the graph: $F \times \Delta t$ (area) $\dfrac{(150 \times 0.09)}{2} = 0.17 \times \Delta v$; $\Delta v = \dfrac{(6.75)}{0.17} = 39.7 = 40\,\text{m s}^{-1}$
6	E	1	Doppler equation. Car is travelling towards a student therefore the frequency will be greater: $f_0 = f_s \dfrac{v}{v - v_s} = 750 \times \dfrac{340}{340 - 25} = 809.5 = 810\,\text{Hz}$
7	B	1	It is the force from the coupling that causes the car's motion: $F = m \times a = 700 \times 2.0 = 1400\,\text{N}$
8	C	1	Box is sliding at a constant velocity. Forces are balanced so friction = $m \times g \times \sin 30 = 19.6\,\text{N}$
9	C	1	First minima means path difference is 0.5λ. $0.5\lambda = 0.6\,\text{m}$; $\lambda = 1.2\,\text{m}$; $f = \dfrac{v}{\lambda} = \dfrac{340}{1.2} = 283\,\text{Hz}$
10	B	1	V_1 is $1.5\,\text{V}$ therefore voltage across variable resistor is $6 - 1.5 = 4.5\,\text{V}$. $I = \dfrac{V}{R} = \dfrac{4.5\,\text{V}}{6000} = 0.75\,\text{mA}$
11	D	1	Energy gained is calculated using $E = qV$. $E = q \times V = 1.6 \times 10^{-19} \times 3000 = 4.8 \times 10^{-16}\,\text{J}$
12	E	1	Two up and one down quark gives a charge of $+\dfrac{2}{3} + \dfrac{2}{3} + -\dfrac{1}{3}$ This gives a charge of +1, therefore proton.
13	D	1	Reading from the graph. No current below f_0. Above f_0 the current increases as the frequency increases (I and II).
14	E	1	Moving charges generate a magnetic field. This field interacts with the plotting compasses and they move.
15	C	1	The angle of incidence is $90 - 55 = 35°$. We then use $\dfrac{\sin i}{\sin r} = \dfrac{\sin 35}{\sin 30} = 1.15$
16	D	1	Refractive index varies with the frequency of the light and this means different frequencies are deviated by different amounts.

Question	Answer	Mark	Commentary with hints and tips
17	A	1	To calculate frequency you need to obtain a value for time for one wave. $T = 4 \times 0 \cdot 008 = 0 \cdot 032$ s. $f = \dfrac{1}{T} = 31 \cdot 25$ Hz. $V_p = 3 \times 0 \cdot 5$ mV $= 1 \cdot 5$ mV $= 0 \cdot 0015$ V
18	A	1	A rearrangement of $E = \dfrac{1}{2} \dfrac{Q^2}{C}$
19	D	1	Using Ohm's law $I = \dfrac{V}{R} = \dfrac{9 \cdot 0}{3 \cdot 0} = 3 \cdot 0$ A $I_p = 3 \cdot 0 \times \sqrt{2} = 4 \cdot 2$ A
20	A	1	Atoms in the outer layers of the Sun absorb photons emanating from the Sun.

Section 2

Question			Expected answer	Maximum mark	Commentary with hints and tips
1	a)	(i)	$E_p = m \times g \times h$ $= 9{\cdot}8 \times 1{\cdot}25 \times 1{\cdot}4 = 17{\cdot}15$ $= 17\,\text{J}$	1 1 1	Straightforward application of the equation
		(ii)	$E_p = E_k$ $17 = \frac{1}{2} \times m \times v^2$ $17 = \frac{1}{2} \times 1{\cdot}25 \times v^2$ $v^2 = \frac{34}{1{\cdot}25} = 27{\cdot}2$ $\sqrt{27{\cdot}2} = 5{\cdot}2\,\text{m s}^{-1}$	1 1 1 1	Conservation of energy. Use energy gain at top of slope to equate to kinetic energy at bottom. All numbers equate to 2 s.f.
	b)	(i)	$v_h = v \times \cos 25°$ $= 4{\cdot}5 \times \cos 25° = 4{\cdot}1\,\text{m s}^{-1}$	1	Resolving velocity into horizontal and vertical components
		(ii)	$v_v = v \times \sin 25°$ $= 4{\cdot}5 \times \sin 25° = 1{\cdot}9\,\text{m s}^{-1}$	1	
		(iii)	$v = u + a \times t$ $-1{\cdot}9 = 1{\cdot}9 + -9{\cdot}8 \times t$ $t = \frac{-3{\cdot}8}{-9{\cdot}8}$ $= 0{\cdot}388\,\text{s}$ Horizontal distance is given by $v_h \times t = 4{\cdot}1 \times 0{\cdot}388 = 1{\cdot}6\,\text{m}$	1 1 1 1	To calculate horizontal distance we need to know how long the projectile is in the air for (t) and its horizontal velocity. To calculate t we need to use our equations of motion and firstly consider the vertical motion. When it returns to the ground its vertical displacement is 0 m. It is back at the same height. Its vertical velocity is −1·9 m s⁻¹ as it will return to the ground at the same velocity.
		(iv)		1 for axes 1 for points	
2	a)		Mass of rocket at take off $= 3550 + 2740 + 1650 + 2150$ $= 10\,090\,\text{kg}$	1	Mass at take off is the mass of all the sections combined
	b)		$a = \frac{F_{un}}{m}$ $F_{un} = 120\,000\,\text{N} - \text{weight}$ $Wt = 10\,090 \times 9{\cdot}8 = 98\,882\,\text{N}$ $120\,000 - 98\,882 = 21\,118\,\text{N}$ $a = \frac{21\,118}{10\,090}$ $= 2{\cdot}1\,\text{m s}^{-2}$	1 1 1 1 1	The unbalanced force is the thrust of the rocket's engine minus the weight of the rocket. Subtract these to get F and then divide by the mass of the rocket.

	Question		Expected answer	Maximum mark	Commentary with hints and tips
	c)		Impulse $= F \times t$ $= 105\,000 \times 25$ $= 2\,625\,000\,\text{Ns}$	1 1 1	Gain in impulse is due to the second stage engine firing for 25 s. This impulse is then used to calculate the gain in velocity.
	d)		It would make no difference to the impulse as this is due to the firing of the second stage engine.	1	
	e)		The change in velocity would be less as the mass of the ship is greater due to the first stage not being ejected.	2	
3	a)		$r = 1\cdot74 \times 10^6 + 1\cdot90 \times 10^5$ $r = 1\cdot93 \times 10^6\,\text{m}$ $r^2 = 3\cdot72 \times 10^{12}$ $F = G\dfrac{m_1 m_2}{r^2}$ $\dfrac{(6\cdot67 \times 10^{-11} \times 7\cdot34 \times 10^{22} \times 28\,400)}{3\cdot72 \times 10^{12}}$ $= 37\,376 = 37\,400\,\text{N}$	1 1 1 1 1	The radius is calculated by adding the radius of the Moon to the height of the module above the surface of the Moon. This is then used in the equation to determine the gravitational force. All answers are to 3 s.f.
	b)		The module would be attracted by the gravitational field of the Moon. With no orbital velocity, it would gradually accelerate towards the surface of the Moon.	1 1	
4			Early cars were made to be strong and sturdy and not easily damaged. This resulted in serious injury for drivers and passengers as they made contact with the vehicle during collisions. Softer materials, air bags and crumple zones are designed to reduce the rate at which the passenger is slowed down. They do this by increasing the time taken for the vehicle to stop. Crumple zones absorb energy and stop the car over a longer time, air bags inflate and reduce the speed of the passenger gradually. If the passenger strikes the dashboard it will be curved (not sharp) and have a degree of padding. All of this is intended to decrease the rate at which the passenger slows down therefore reducing the force on impact.	3, 2, 1	Open ended question based on 3, 2, 1 or 0 marks. The marks are given on a scale of a good, reasonable and poor knowledge of physics in explaining the topic.

B

	Question		Expected answer	Maximum mark	Commentary with hints and tips
5	a)		Mass of three carriages $= 3 \times 1450 = 4350\,kg$ Mass of engine $= 2750\,kg$ Total mass $= 7100\,kg$ $a = \dfrac{F}{m}$ $= \dfrac{6500}{7100} = 0 \cdot 92\,m\,s^{-2}$	1 1 1 1	
	b)		$F = m \times a$ $= 4350 \times 0 \cdot 92$ $= 4002 = 4000\,N$	1 1	
	c)		Less mass would result in a greater acceleration. This resultant drop in friction would also allow a greater top speed.	1 1	Removing a carriage would increase the initial acceleration of the train. The mass of the train has decreased and the force has remained constant; therefore the initial acceleration would be greater. The top speed of the train would also increase; this is determined by the force from the engine being balanced by the friction and drag of the train. With a carriage removed there will be less friction so the train should be able to reach a higher speed at the same output.
6	a)		To direct the particles and to ensure they follow the correct path	1	
	b)		To accelerate the particles	1	
	c)		$E = 75\,MeV$ $= 75 \times 10^6 \times 1 \cdot 6 \times 10^{-19}\,J$ $= 1 \cdot 2 \times 10^{-11}\,J$ $E_k = \dfrac{1}{2} \times m \times v^2$ $1 \cdot 2 \times 10^{-11} = \dfrac{1}{2} \times 1 \cdot 673 \times 10^{-27} \times v^2$ $v^2 = \dfrac{2 \times 1 \cdot 2 \times 10^{-11}}{1 \cdot 673 \times 10^{-27}}$ $= 1 \cdot 43 \times 10^{16}$ $v = 1 \cdot 2 \times 10^8\,m\,s^{-1}$	1 1 1 1 1	Convert MeV to joules Equate the gain in energy to be converted to kinetic energy. Solve for v.
	d)		It would double the energy of the particle. This would lead to an increase in velocity by a factor of 1·4 as v varies as $\sqrt{\text{energy}}$.	1 1	$E_k \propto v^2$ This velocity is so high there will start to be some relativistic effects but the question is specifically asking about energy and its relationship to velocity.

Question			Expected answer	Maximum mark	Commentary with hints and tips
7	a)		$E = q \times v$ $E = 1{\cdot}6 \times 10^{-19} \times 60\,000$ $\quad = 9{\cdot}6 \times 10^{-15}\,J$ $E_k = \frac{1}{2} \times m \times v^2$ $9{\cdot}6 \times 10^{-15} = \frac{1}{2} \times 1{\cdot}673 \times 10^{-27} \times v^2$ $v^2 = \dfrac{2 \times 9{\cdot}6 \times 10^{-15}}{1{\cdot}673 \times 10^{-27}}$ $v^2 = 1{\cdot}147 \times 10^{13}$ $v = 3{\cdot}4 \times 10^6\,m\,s^{-1}$	1 1 1 1	Equate the gain in energy to be converted to kinetic energy. Solve for v.
	b)			Axes 1 Graph with horizontal 1 and sloping steps 1	The graph should show regular increases in energy. The proton increases its energy every time it passes across the electric field. Each crossing equates to a sloping line on the graph.
8	a)		In a fission reaction more massive nuclei are separated or 'split' to form smaller nuclei. The total mass of the smaller nuclei is less than that of the original atom. This 'excess' mass is converted to energy and is used to generate electricity in power stations.	1 1 1	Straightforward description of fission reaction highlighting a change in mass which is then converted to energy.
	b)		Mass before reaction $5{\cdot}00827 \times 10^{-27}\,kg + 5{\cdot}00827 \times 10^{-27}\,kg = 1{\cdot}001654 \times 10^{-26}\,kg$ Mass after reaction $6{\cdot}64648 \times 10^{-27} + 2 \times 1{\cdot}67493 \times 10^{-27} = 9{\cdot}99634 \times 10^{-27}\,kg$ Difference in mass $= 2{\cdot}02 \times 10^{-29}\,kg$ Energy $= m \times c^2$ $\qquad = 2{\cdot}02 \times 10^{-29} \times (3 \times 10^8)^2$ $\qquad = 1{\cdot}818 \times 10^{-12}\,J$ $\qquad = 1{\cdot}82 \times 10^{-12}\,J$	1 1 1 1	
	c)		In a fusion reaction there is less radioactive waste. This means there are fewer issues associated with decontamination and storage of low-level waste.	1 1	It is difficult to comment fully on this as there are only a few fusion reactors in operation. There is less radioactive waste but there may be issues regarding the radiation released during the reaction.

	Question		Expected answer	Maximum mark	Commentary with hints and tips
9	a)		Lost volts $= Ir$ $3 \cdot 1 = 65 \times r$ $r = \dfrac{3 \cdot 1}{65}$ $= 0 \cdot 048 = 0 \cdot 05 \,\Omega$	1 1 1	Take the open reading as the e.m.f. and use this to determine the lost volts. This is then used to give a value for r.
	b)		When the leads touch, they are effectively short circuiting the battery. This means that all the voltage is across the internal resistance of the battery. This produces a very high current due to $I = \dfrac{E}{r} = \dfrac{12 \cdot 3}{0 \cdot 05} = 246\,A$ This can generate the sparks.	1 1	
	c)		With a normal operating current of 65 A, a thin cable would overheat. In order to survive such high loads, a thick cable is required.	1 1	
	d)		Connect capacitor to battery and when voltage across capacitor reaches a constant value, the capacitor is fully charged.	1 1	Capacitor is fully charged when voltage reaches a constant value.
	e)		Connect the ammeter in series with the capacitor and switch on. When ammeter reading drops to zero, the capacitor is fully charged	1 1	When capacitor is at same voltage as the supply then no p.d. therefore no current flows
	f)		$I = \dfrac{V}{R}$ $\dfrac{12 \cdot 3}{85}$ $= 0 \cdot 14\,A$	1 1 1	
	g)		The initial current would be smaller as there is a larger resistance in the circuit. The smaller current would mean it would take longer to discharge.	1 1	Simple charging and discharging of a small capacitor circuit

	Question		Expected answer	Maximum mark	Commentary with hints and tips
10			$r = \dfrac{\sin i}{\sin r}$ $1\cdot4 = \dfrac{\sin 45}{\sin r}$ $\sin r = \dfrac{\sin 45}{1\cdot4}$ $\qquad = 0\cdot505$ $r = 30°$	1 1 1	Ensure that the correct value for i is used; however in this example it is not important as $i = 45°$
			Calculation of angles at bottom of prism. Determination of angles at first boundary Determination of angles at second boundary	1 1	$r = 30°$; the angle between ray and prism wall is $60°$. This means that the ray makes an angle of $55°$ with the bottom face of the prism. This means the internal angle of incidence is $35°$. Many candidates find this difficult but it is a relatively simple calculation of the angles in a triangle at the bottom of the prism
			$\sin\dfrac{\sin 35}{\sin r} = \dfrac{1}{1\cdot4}$ $\sin 35 \times 1\cdot4 = \sin r = 0\cdot803$ $r = 53\cdot4 = 53°$	1 1 1	
11	a)		$d \sin\theta = m\lambda$ $\quad \sin\theta = \dfrac{m\lambda}{d}$ $\qquad = \dfrac{2 \times 565 \times 10^{-9}}{3\cdot5 \times 10^{-6}}$ $\qquad = 0\cdot322$ $\qquad = 18\cdot8° = 19°$	1 1 1 1	m is 2 as it is the 2nd order being calculated
	b)		As the detector moves from X to Y it will cut across two 'lines' of constructive interference and two 'lines' of destructive interference.	1 1	In this question you are asked to cut across horizontally rather than vertically. If you imagine the lines of interference emanating from the centre, you will cut through these as the detector travels across.

	Question		Expected answer	Maximum mark	Commentary with hints and tips
12	a)		To convert light years to m we multiple the distance (ly) by $365 \cdot 25 \times 24 \times 60 \times 60 \times 3 \times 10^8$ e.g $1 \cdot 40 \times 10^9$ ly becomes $1 \cdot 33 \times 10^{25}$ s Distances are (m): $9 \cdot 47 \times 10^{24}$ $1 \cdot 33 \times 10^{25}$ $2 \cdot 37 \times 10^{25}$	3	This is a data handling exercise involving the use of large numbers. There are a number of complex calculations involving conversions and the frequent use of scientific notation. The question uses 3 s.f. so answer to 3 s.f.
	b)		Velocities are (m s^{-1}) $1 \cdot 50 \times 10^7$ $2 \cdot 20 \times 10^7$ $3 \cdot 90 \times 10^7$	2	The velocities are more easily converted by multiplying by 1000.
	c)		 $M = \dfrac{(y_2 - y_1)}{(x_2 - x_1)}$ $\dfrac{(3 \cdot 90 - 1 \cdot 50) \times 10^7)}{2 \cdot 37 \times 10^{25} - 9 \cdot 47 \times 10^{24}}$ $= 1 \cdot 686 \times 10^{-18}$ $= 1 \cdot 69 \times 10^{-18}$	3	A common way to do this would be to draw a graph of recessional velocity (ms^{-1}) versus distance (m). The calculation of the slope will give a value for Hubble's constant using these data.
	d)		Time $= \dfrac{1}{H_0}$ $\dfrac{1}{1 \cdot 69 \times 10^{-18}}$ $= 5 \cdot 92 \times 10^{17}$ s	2	All of the question has 3 s.f. so answer to 3 s.f.

C

Practice Paper C

Section 1

Question	Answer	Mark	Commentary with hints and tips
1	D	1	Gradient is negative, so downward vector direction is negative. Ground contact is when velocity vector changes to positive.
2	B	1	Between B and C the speed is decreasing therefore the net force is upwards, i.e. weight force < upthrust.
3	B	1	Pythagoras gives magnitude of 8·6 N. Trigonometry gives the angle as 36° above the 7 N vector so 054 as a bearing.
4	D	1	$P = \dfrac{E}{t} = \dfrac{mgh}{t} = \dfrac{3\cdot5 \times 9.8 \times 2.4}{30} = 2\cdot74\,\text{W (watts)}$
5	B	1	Total momentum before the explosion = total momentum after (in the absence of an external force), $p = mv$. If the velocity of one fragment is twice that of the other but in the opposite direction, then the mass of the second must be half that of the first.
6	D	1	For projectiles, horizontal velocity is constant as horizontal acceleration is zero (ignoring air resistance). Vertical velocity is constantly changing as vertical acceleration is non-zero.
7	C	1	The speed of light in a vacuum is the same for all observers.
8	B	1	$z = \dfrac{\Delta\lambda}{\lambda_{rest}} = \dfrac{700 - 630}{630} = 0\cdot111$
9	E	1	We can estimate the mass of a galaxy by the orbital speed of stars within it.
10	E	1	Fermions, the matter particles, consist of quarks (six types) and leptons (electron, muon and tau, together with their neutrinos). The force-mediating particles are bosons (photons, W and Z bosons, and gluons).
11	A	1	$E = hf = 6\cdot63 \times 10^{-34} \times 9\cdot5 \times 10^{14} = 6\cdot30 \times 10^{-19}$ $E_k = 6\cdot29 \times 10^{-19}\,\text{J} - 5\cdot2 \times 10^{-19}\,\text{J} = 1\cdot09 \times 10^{-19}\,\text{J} = 1\cdot1 \times 10^{-19}\,\text{J}$ The energy of the photon is able to eject the electron and its 'surplus' energy is transferred to the electron.
12	E	1	An electric field enables free charges to move. Answers I and II are meaningless statements.
13	D	1	The photon enables the electron to move bands.
14	D	1	$I \times d^2 = k$ Choose a set of values. $5\cdot2 \times 0\cdot15^2 = 0\cdot117$ $I = \dfrac{0\cdot117}{1\cdot1^2} = 0\cdot097$
15	B	1	The rotation of the galaxies is not what was anticipated. The suggested explanation is that there is some form of matter which allows for this.

Question	Answer	Mark	Commentary with hints and tips
16	C	1	The ray alters direction towards the normal between the prisms therefore B has greater refractive index.
17	A	1	A lower energy means a lower frequency which in turn means a greater wavelength.
18	E	1	$m\lambda = d \sin \theta$; $\sin \theta = \dfrac{m\lambda}{d}$ Make λ larger and d smaller to increase separation.
19	D	1	$E = \frac{1}{2}CV^2 = \frac{1}{2} \times 46 \times 10^{-6} \times (15^2 - 9^2) = 3 \cdot 3 \times 10^{-3}\,\text{J}$
20	B	1	$\rho = \dfrac{RA}{l}$; $R = \dfrac{\rho l}{A} = \dfrac{6 \cdot 2 \times 10^{-8} \times 65}{\pi \times 0 \cdot 005^2}$ $\quad = 0 \cdot 051\,\Omega = 0 \cdot 05\,\Omega$

Section 2

Question			Expected response	Maximum mark	Commentary with hints and tips
1	a)	(i)	$H = 225 \times \sin 60 = 194\cdot9\,\text{m (W)}$ $V = 225 \cos 60 = 112\cdot5\,\text{m (N)}$ This gives a total of $175 + 112\cdot5\,\text{m}$ $= 287\cdot5\,\text{m N}$ and $194\cdot9\,\text{m W}$ Displacement $= \sqrt{(287\cdot5^2 + 194\cdot9^2)}$ $= \sqrt{120\,642} = 347\,\text{m}$ Direction $= \tan^{-1}\left|\dfrac{194\cdot9}{287\cdot5}\right| = 34\degree\,\text{W}$ of N	1 1 1 1	175 m N then 225 m 60° West of North. Part 1 of journey is 175 m N. Part 2 requires the journey to be resolved into horizontal and vertical components which are displacements in the northern and western directions.
		(ii)	velocity $= \dfrac{\text{displacement}}{\text{time}}$ $= \dfrac{347}{140}$ $= 2\cdot5\,\text{ms}^{-1}$ on a bearing of 326°	1 1	
	b)		speed $= \dfrac{\text{distance}}{\text{time}}$ $= 175 + 225 + 347$ $= \dfrac{747}{250} = 3\,\text{m s}^{-1}$	1 1 1	The distance here is the sum of all the distances travelled by the drone. The displacement in this case would be zero.
2	a)	(i)	$s = ut + \dfrac{1}{2}at^2$ as $u = 0$ $s = \dfrac{1}{2}at^2$ $1\cdot75 = \dfrac{1}{2} \times 9\cdot8 \times t^2$ $t^2 = \dfrac{1\cdot75 \times 2}{9\cdot8} = 0\cdot357$ $t = 0\cdot597 = 0\cdot60\,\text{s}$	1 1 1	Ball is dropped therefore $u = 0$. Select appropriate relationship from list. g is given to 2 s.f. so our answer should be to 2 s.f.
		(ii)	$v = u + at$ $v = 9\cdot8 \times 0\cdot6$ $= 5\cdot9\,\text{m s}^{-1}$	1 1 1	Knowing t we can use this simple relationship.
	b)	(i)	$v^2 = u^2 + 2as$ $0 = u^2 + 2 \times -9\cdot8 \times 1\cdot23$ $u^2 = 24\cdot108$ $u = 4\cdot9\,\text{m s}^{-1}$	1 1 1	Height reached is 1·23 m and vertical velocity at that point = $0\,\text{m s}^{-1}$

	Question		Expected response	Maximum mark	Commentary with hints and tips
		(ii)	Time to bounce up (and also to return) $v = u + at; 0 = 4\cdot9 - 9\cdot8 \times t$ $t = \dfrac{4\cdot9}{9\cdot8} = 0\cdot5\,s$ Total time is $0\cdot5 + 0\cdot5 = 1\cdot0\,s$	1 1 1	Again, at top of bounce $v = 0\,m\,s^{-1}$. Time to rise and fall again. If it takes $0\cdot5\,s$ to rise it will also take $0\cdot5\,s$ to fall.
	c)		Correct axes and scales Correct units Correct insertion of points and connecting line 	1 1 1	
3	a)		In the XY direction Tug 1: $F = 40\cdot0 \times 10^3 \times \cos(25) = 3\cdot63 \times 10^4$ Tug 2: $F = 40\cdot0 \times 10^3 \times \cos(-15)$ $= 3\cdot86 \times 10^4$ Total $= 7\cdot49 \times 10^4\,N$ *to the right* Perpendicular to XY Tug 1: $F = 40\cdot0 \times 10^3 \times \sin(25) = 1\cdot69 \times 10^4$ Tug 2: $F = 40\cdot0 \times 10^3 \times \sin(-15)$ $= -1\cdot04 \times 10^4$ Total $= 6\cdot5 \times 10^3\,N$ *up the page* Pythagoras gives resultant magnitude: $F = \sqrt{(7\cdot49^3 + 0\cdot65^2)} \times 10^4$ $F = 7\cdot518 \times 10^4\,N$ $F = 7\cdot52 \times 10^4\,N$	1 1 1 1	Resolve the two vectors into perpendicular components: along the direction XY and perpendicular to XY. Add the components for each direction, taking account of +/– directions. Use Pythagoras to find the resultant magnitude. The sine and cosine rules may be used if the candidate is familiar with these approaches. Poorest significant figure in the question is 3 s.f., so answer to 3 s.f.
	b)		$\tan\theta = \dfrac{\text{perpendicular}}{\text{parallel}}$ $\tan\theta = \dfrac{6\cdot5 \times 10^3}{7\cdot52 \times 10^4}$ $\theta = \tan^{-1}(8\cdot6436 \times 10^{-2})$ $\theta = 4\cdot94°$ above the line XY	1 1 1	Any trig function may be used. The answer must include the reference direction (i.e. the XY line).

	Question		Expected response	Maximum mark	Commentary with hints and tips
	c)		$F = ma$ $7 \cdot 52 \times 10^4 = 2 \cdot 84 \times 10^6 \times a$ $a = 2 \cdot 6479 \times 10^{-2}\,m\,s^{-2}$ $a = 2 \cdot 65 \times 10^{-2}\,m\,s^{-2}$ at $4 \cdot 94°$ above the line XY	1 1 1	Poorest significant figure in the question is 3 s.f., so answer to 3 s.f. Answer MUST include vector direction.
	d)		Other resistive/frictional forces will act on both tug and tanker to oppose the forward motion.	1	All moving objects experience friction in reality.
4	a)		$F = \dfrac{G\,m_1 m_2}{r^2}$ $F = \dfrac{6 \cdot 67 \times 10^{-11} \times 5 \cdot 97 \times 10^{24} \times 7 \cdot 35 \times 10^{22}}{(3 \cdot 85 \times 10^8)^2}$ $F = 1 \cdot 9745 \times 10^{20}\,N$ $F = 1 \cdot 97 \times 10^{20}\,N$	1 1 1	Do not forget to convert km to m. It's very common for candidates to forget to square the distance. Poorest significant figure in the question is 3 s.f., so answer to 3 s.f.
	b)		The force acts along the vector connecting the centre of mass of the Moon and the centre of mass of the Earth (i.e. along the radius vector).	1	
	c)		$\sqrt{\dfrac{M_e}{M_m}} = \dfrac{R}{r_m} - 1$ $\sqrt{\dfrac{5 \cdot 97 \times 10^{24}}{7 \cdot 35 \times 10^{22}}} = \dfrac{3 \cdot 85 \times 10^8}{r_m} - 1$ $r_m = \dfrac{3 \cdot 85 \times 10^8}{9 \cdot 0125 + 1}$ $r_m = 3 \cdot 8452 \times 10^7$ $r_m = 3 \cdot 85 \times 10^7\,m$	1 1 1	This is a typical 'can you use a new equation?' type of question. Insert the numbers from the question and rearrange to solve. Poorest significant figure in the question is 3 s.f., so answer to 3 s.f.

Question			Expected response	Maximum mark	Commentary with hints and tips
5			Hubble found a relationship of direct proportion between the distance from Earth of an observed galaxy and the velocity of the galaxy. Distances (d) were calculated using the parallax method and velocities (v) were calculated using Doppler red-shift observations. Graphing this data gave a best-fit line with constant gradient which passed through the origin of the graph and allowed Hubble to propose that a law existed such that $v = Hd$, where H is the gradient of the line, i.e. the constant of proportionality. This constant has dimensions of $\frac{1}{\text{time}}$ and so may be used to estimate the age of the Universe, where age $= \frac{1}{H}$. In addition, the facts that all galaxies are moving away from each other and that the more distant ones are moving more quickly leads to a thought experiment of 'reversing time' – playing the expanding Universe backwards suggests that all galaxies originated from a single point and gives rise to the possibility of a 'Big Bang' theory of a single point of Universe origin.	3	Demonstrates no understanding: 0 marks. Demonstrates limited understanding: 1 mark. Demonstrates reasonable understanding: 2 marks. Demonstrates good understanding: 3 marks. This is an open-ended question. 1 mark: The student has demonstrated a limited understanding of the physics involved. The student has made some statement(s) which is/are relevant to the situation, showing that at least a little of the physics within the problem is understood. 2 marks: The student has demonstrated a reasonable understanding of the physics involved. The student makes some statement(s) which is/are relevant to the situation, showing that the problem is understood. 3 marks: The maximum available mark would be awarded to a student who has demonstrated a good understanding of the physics involved. The student shows a good comprehension of the physics of the situation and has provided a logically correct answer to the question posed. This type of response might include a statement of the principles involved, a relationship or an equation, and the application of these to respond to the problem. This does not mean the answer has to be what might be termed an 'excellent' answer or a 'complete' one.
6	a)		$T = \dfrac{2 \cdot 898 \times 10^{-3}}{\lambda_{\text{peak}}}$ $= \dfrac{2 \cdot 898 \times 10^{-3}}{5 \cdot 05 \times 10^{-9}}$ $= 5 \cdot 74 \times 10^{5}\,\text{K}$	1 1 1	Smallest s.f. is 3 s.f. so answer given to 3 s.f.

	Question		Expected response	Maximum mark	Commentary with hints and tips
	b)	(i)	$T = \dfrac{2\cdot898 \times 10^{-3}}{\lambda_{peak}}$ $\lambda_{peak} = \dfrac{2\cdot898 \times 10^{-3}}{2\cdot0}$ $= 0\cdot001449 = 1\cdot45 \times 10^{-3}\,m$	1 1 1	Keeping to 3 sig. figs for final answer.
		(ii)	This is in the microwave radiation band. It was proposed that this radiation would be present as a result of the expansion of the Universe and when it was detected, it provided very strong evidence in support of the Big Bang theory.	1 1 1	
7	a)		The nuclear decay is a quantum process and so always involves the same energy change. If the beta particle has a range of energies then there must be another, difficult to detect (low mass and uncharged) particle, i.e. the neutrino.	1 1	
	b)		From the graph, most common energy is $0\cdot05\,MeV$ $E_k = 0\cdot05 \times 1\cdot6 \times 10^{-13}\,J$ $E_k = 8\cdot0 \times 10^{-15}\,J$ $E_k = \frac{1}{2}mv^2$ $8\cdot0 \times 10^{-15} = \frac{1}{2} \times 9\cdot11 \times 10^{-31}v^2$ $v = \sqrt{\left(\dfrac{16 \times 10^{-15}}{9\cdot11 \times 10^{-31}}\right)}$ $v = 1\cdot3253 \times 10^8\,m\,s^{-1}$ $v = 1\cdot3 \times 10^8\,m\,s^{-1}$	1 1 1 1	Read from the graph, preferably by using a ruler to draw a vertical line to intersect the x-axis. Forgetting to square root (or other error) will likely give $> 3 \times 10^8\,m\,s^{-1}$, which is impossible (good cross check). Poorest significant figure in the question is 2 s.f., so answer to 2 s.f.
8	a)		Any wavelength shorter then green (e.g. blue, violet, UV). This will mean the frequency is higher and so the energy of each photon $(E = hf)$ is larger. If the photon energy is larger than the work function, a current will be detected.	1 1 1	
	b)		$E = hf$ $2\cdot8 \times 10^{-19} = 6\cdot63 \times 10^{-34} \times f$ $f = 4\cdot2232 \times 10^{14}\,Hz$ $f = 4\cdot2 \times 10^{14}\,Hz$	1 1 1	The work function must just be equal to the energy of the incoming photon. Poorest significant figure in the question is 2 s.f., so answer to 2 s.f.

	Question		Expected response	Maximum mark	Commentary with hints and tips
9	a)		First minimum – path difference $=\frac{1}{2}\lambda = 0.5\,cm$ $\lambda = 1\,cm$	1 1	
	b)		$m\lambda = d\sin\theta$ $0.01 = 0.045 \times \sin\theta$ $\sin\theta = \dfrac{0.01}{0.045} = 0.22$ $\theta = 12.8 = 13\,°$	1 1 1 1	
10	a)		$E = qV$ $1.6 \times 10^{-19} \times 2500$ $= 4.0 \times 10^{-16}\,J$	1 1 1	Answer given to 2 sig. figs
	b)		$E = \frac{1}{2}mv^2$ $4.0 \times 10^{-16} = \frac{1}{2} \times 2.8 \times 10^{-25} \times v^2$ $v^2 = \dfrac{2 \times 4.0 \times 10^{-16}}{2.8 \times 10^{-25}}$ $v^2 = 2.857 \times 10^9$ $v = 5.3 \times 10^5\,m\,s^{-1}$	1 1 1	Equating electrical energy gain to kinetic energy of ion
	c)		$F \times \Delta t = m \times \Delta v$ $F \times 90 = 0.0002 \times 5.3 \times 10^5$ $F = \dfrac{0.0002 \times 5.3 \times 10^5}{90} = 1.17 = 1.2\,N$	1 1 1	Again answer consistent with 2 s.f.
11	a)		Irradiance is the power of the source per unit area.	1	The definition comes directly from the equation $I = \dfrac{P}{A}$. P: power; A: unit area; / means 'per'
	b)		Given the relationship $I = \dfrac{k}{d^2}$, the data need to be processed to calculate $\dfrac{1}{d^2}$. A graph of I vs $\dfrac{1}{d^2}$ will be a straight line through the origin (i.e. directly proportional).	1 1	
	c)		Stray light from the room would affect the results; the graph of I vs $\dfrac{1}{d^2}$ would not pass through the origin because of this systematic error (uncertainty).	1	

	Question		Expected response	Maximum mark	Commentary with hints and tips
12	a)		The light emitted by a star is a continuous spectrum. As that light passes through the gases in the atmosphere of the star, specific wavelengths are absorbed by the atoms (molecules) of gas.	1 1	
	b)		$f = \dfrac{3 \times 10^8}{656 \cdot 2 \times 10^9}$ $E = hf$ $E = \dfrac{6 \cdot 63 \times 10^{-34} \times 3 \times 10^8}{656 \cdot 2 \times 10^{-9}}$ $E = 3 \cdot 03109 \times 10^{-19}\,J$ $E = 3 \cdot 031 \times 10^{-19}\,J$	1 1 1 1	Minimum energy = smallest frequency = largest wavelength = $H\alpha$ Poorest significant figure in the question is 4 s.f., so answer to 4 s.f.
13	a)		 Axes and units appropriately scaled y-axis: volts (V) going up to 10 V x-axis: current (I) going up to 4 A Correct insertion of all points	1 1 2	
	b)	(i)	Extend graph to intersect y–axis to give $E = 9 \cdot 0\,V$	1	
		(ii)	Calculate slope of graph to determine internal resistance $m = \dfrac{(y_2 - y_1)}{(x_2 - x_1)}$ $= \dfrac{(8 \cdot 0 - 5 \cdot 8)}{(1 \cdot 0 - 2 \cdot 9)}$ $= \dfrac{2 \cdot 2}{-1 \cdot 9} = -1 \cdot 2$ The gradient of the graph is $-r = -1 \cdot 2$ therefore $r = 1 \cdot 2\,\Omega$	1 1 1	Acceptable to draw best fitting straight line and take two points, one from either end of graph. Suggested answer chose two points from data. Again 2 s.f.

	Question		Expected response	Maximum mark	Commentary with hints and tips
14	a)	(i)	$V = IR_{total}$ $12{\cdot}0 = 1{\cdot}22 \times 10^{-3} \times R_{total}$ $R_{total} = 9836$ $R_V = 9836 - 4400$ $R_V = 5436 - 5440\,\Omega$	1 1 1	
		(ii)	$V = IR$ $V = 1{\cdot}22 \times 10^{-3} \times 5440$ $V = 6{\cdot}637$ $V = 6{\cdot}64\,V$	1 1 1	There are a number of ways of answering this question but this was chosen as it breaks down the calculations into relatively simple and straightforward steps.
	b)	(i)	$\dfrac{1}{R_t} = \dfrac{1}{R_1} + \dfrac{1}{R_2}$ $= \dfrac{1}{4400} + \dfrac{1}{1300} = 9{\cdot}965 \times 10^{-4}$ $R_t = 1003 = 1000\,\Omega$	1 1 1	
		(ii)	This will increase the voltage across the variable resistor. The resistance of the parallel resistors will be less than $4400\,\Omega$. There will be less voltage across this section. Therefore more voltage across the variable resistor.	1 1	